30
PROPERTIES
BEFORE
30

30 PROPERTIES BEFORE 30

HOW YOU CAN START INVESTING IN PROPERTY RIGHT NOW

EDDIE DILLEEN

WILEY

First published in 2022 by John Wiley & Sons Australia, Ltd

42 McDougall St, Milton Qld 4064
Office also in Melbourne

Typeset in Adobe Caslon Pro 11pt/15pt

ISBN: 978-0-730-39989-6

A catalogue record for this book is available from the National Library of Australia

Cover design by Wiley

Cover and internal image © Jandrie Lombard/Shutterstock

Disclaimer
The material in this publication is of the nature of general comment only, and does not represent professional advice. It is not intended to provide specific guidance for particular circumstances and it should not be relied on as the basis for any decision to take action or not take action on any matter which it covers. Readers should obtain professional advice where appropriate, before making any such decision. To the maximum extent permitted by law, the author and publisher disclaim all responsibility and liability to any person, arising directly or indirectly from any person taking or not taking action based on the information in this publication.

Printed in Singapore
M WEP322393 041124

*This book is dedicated to my mother,
Elizabeth Dilleen. Without her I would not have
grown into the man I am today.*

CONTENTS

INTRODUCTION

I have written this book to inspire and educate readers interested in creating wealth and reaching their financial goals through property investment in Australia.

I'll walk you through my strategy for property investment success, step by step. I've dedicated thousands of hours and battled in the trenches to develop this strategy, which has made millions of dollars for me and my clients, and will continue to do so into the future.

This investment strategy is extremely powerful for three core reasons:

1. It works fast, meaning in three to seven years (note well: *there is no magic get-rich-quick formula*). It's unlike the transitional property investment strategy most Aussies apply, which is to buy and then either hope and pray the market rises over time or get their hands dirty doing a bit of renovation to increase equity.

2. It can be used time and time again. It's not a one-time strategy that depends on having the right property, location, size and features. It can be applied to any property, from the most modest to the grandest, in any location and at any time.

3. It can be replicated again and again, because it depends on minimal deposits and makes the money do the work, not you!

So how is this book different? First, I am crazy passionate, even downright obsessed with property investment, as you'll discover. I want to inspire you to reach for what you want in life, and to show you how property investment can get you there.

Second, I have read just about every book out there written by an Australian property investor—you name it and I've read it. And most other authors don't actually share how many properties they have bought or, even more important, whether they still own them and how this has contributed to their financial position. Most of these books are produced by people in their forties and fifties who don't tell us much about their own property deals. What did the figures look like? How did they help them achieve financial freedom? Are they investing in property today or simply reciting strategies they learned five, ten or 20 years ago when property values were half what they are today?

I grew up with a single mother whose only source of income was a government pension. We lived in public housing in one of Sydney's most impoverished neighbourhoods: Mount Druitt. I'll never forget where we came from—the housing commission, food stamps, Salvos furniture and clothes, the endless arguments, tears, stress and embarrassment around the lack of money. I'm sharing this with you so you know I started at the bottom. While most property investors out there had family help in the form of finance or advice, no one in my family even owned their *own* home, let alone an investment property. Many people we grew up around didn't have stable jobs either. Everyone was either renting or living in public housing and struggling to pay their bills and put food on the table.

A common attitude shared by my friends and me growing up was that anyone with money was likely doing something either illegal or immoral, or had inherited it from rich parents. I thought it was impossible for someone like me, without resources or connections, to make money and create wealth—to change the cards I'd been dealt. But I discovered I was wrong. Part of me knows that if it wasn't for our struggle and financial pain, I wouldn't have been inspired to take the massive action I did.

Over the past ten years I've been on a property investment journey, a mission to transform my family's situation. The fire in my belly was sparked by the frustration, pain and feeling of hopelessness of growing up poor.

From starting out living in a housing commission rental in Willmot, Mount Druitt, making an annual wage of less than $26 000, I now have a property portfolio valued in excess of $12 million. With an annual rental income of more than $600 000, that's over $10 000 gross per week. In this book I'm going to share as much as I can of my amazing journey in order to help you achieve your own goals!

I've always been quite competitive, in sports and in many other areas of life. For me the property investment game is no different. If you're to make a success of it, you must be willing to work hard, but first you need to learn and understand it, and one place to start is to read books like this.

Successful property investing generates a snowball effect: for most people it starts slowly, but when using the right strategy, the momentum builds and your portfolio soon gets bigger faster!

Over the past few years, I have used the knowledge I've accumulated to help many others invest in property. You can learn more about this on our website, dilleenproperty.com.au, or watch some of the thousands of hours of free property investment videos on our YouTube channel, Dilleenproperty.

Property investment is my passion (along with basketball—go Lakers!). I have dedicated my life to it. I hope this book ignites a fire in your belly and inspires you to begin your journey or adds fuel to the wealth-creation fire you're already tending! My journey has not been easy, but I have learned so much along the way. This book provides all the information and resources you need to create the life you really want.

PART I

MY STORY

As you'll already have gathered from my background, I'm not your typical property investor, and perhaps partly for this reason, over the years my story and strategies have been featured by multiple media outlets. Many people have reached out to tell me how my story inspired them. Because if I could do it with my initial disadvantages, they realised, then surely they could too. This feedback always makes my day! So after some consideration I decided to begin this book with a brief account of my own personal story.

My message here is simple: it's to never allow the personal challenges you start out with determine the trajectory of the rest of your life. Whatever your circumstances, your future is not set in stone. Only you have the power to create it.

If you have grown up around motivated people who work hard in a stable job and provide for their family, you are luckier than you might realise. But if not, it's never too late to break the cycle. Resisting societal expectations and peer pressures is not easy, nor is breaking poor cross-generational financial habits. Taking control of your life and educating yourself is the first step.

If you want to dive straight into the nitty-gritty of property investing, feel free to flick to Part II. If you'd like to learn a bit about my upbringing and the journey of acquiring my first ten properties (with all figures and details), then read on.

CHAPTER 1
Breaking the cycle

My parents met in Escondido in southern California and got married in their early twenties. My mum had grown up there, the youngest of three siblings, in an average American lower-middle-class family. There wasn't much money. She finished high school but never went to university. No one in my entire family had been to university. I didn't even know what university was until my teens.

My father grew up in Brooklyn, New York. When he was 17 years old he enlisted in the navy, lying about his age. He was sent to Vietnam, where he was wounded and got a silver star for saving others' lives. Mum told me he had a lot of problems after he came home.

Thirteen years after getting married, they moved from the US to Sydney. My father had big dreams of getting rich through multi-level marketing schemes and various other plans, but they never seemed to work out. Dad was a self-employed welder. Later he worked for a company, but the pay was very low. He always wanted more. At the dinner table he'd say how we should always save 10 per cent of what we earn so we could build up a good amount of savings in 10 years. He really wanted to get ahead financially, but no matter what he tried, he just didn't get there. Even when my parents were together and very poor, Dad faced a massive tax debt when he tried to work on his own.

My parents had three children. I was the youngest, born much later than my sister and brother when Dad was 45 and Mum 41. I remember lots of financial stress—my parents were always fighting about money.

Hard times

We lived in a rough area in Mount Druitt. For those unfamiliar with it, Mount Druitt is a lower socioeconomic suburb an hour's drive west of the CBD that has long held a reputation for crime, drugs and domestic violence. But it was affordable and my parents were able to buy a house there in the late 1980s for $50000 and settled into their new life. We lived right next to the shops in the neighbourhood of Whalan. I recall how we were forbidden even to pick up the mail because drug syringes often littered the ground.

My parents split up when I was eight. My father moved to Adelaide and my mum, sister and I moved to Austin, Texas, where Mum's sister lived. My brother stayed in Australia. We arrived in the US with just $300.

The family home was sold for $80000. That house is now worth more than $500000. If they hadn't sold it, our lives could have turned out very differently.

In Austin, Mum got a job as a secretary for an airline. We lived in an ugly two-bedroom unit in another very rough area. My sister had one bedroom and Mum and I shared the other, but we only had one bed in there so Mum would sleep on a pull-out couch. When I would ask for a toy, I was told no, we had to put food on the table.

We didn't have a car at first, so for about six months we had to walk miles to the store and back carrying all our groceries. People would yell out at us through their car windows. When I look back now, it's amusing, but at the time it caused a lot of pain for me. To help Mum, I'd take out the neighbours' rubbish for a dollar or two. I thought that was great!

When I was 12 we returned to Sydney. After the September 11 terror attacks, Mum feared for our safety, especially as she still worked for an airline. We landed in Sydney, and once again Mum had only a few hundred dollars and no job, house or assets. A local church allowed us to stay in a church-owned house until she pulled together enough money to rent our own place. But for a single mum in her mid-fifties, finding work was tough and she had to support us on a modest pension. After a long wait, we were finally approved for a housing commission house in Willmot, another suburb of Mount Druitt.

I still remember seeing the house for the first time. I wasn't expecting a palace, but this place was truly awful. There was a scrawl of graffiti on the back wall, the carpets were old and worn, and a distinct smell of mould permeated the place. Everything was in a sorry state of disrepair. The thought of calling this home filled me with despair. I remember begging Mum not to make us live there, but with private rentals in the area averaging more than $250 a week we had no choice. Mum's pension was only $180 a week. At $65 a week, this subsidised place was all we could afford.

Willmot was rough. There were 'domestic disturbances' every other night. Police cars regularly patrolled the streets and helicopters buzzed overhead. When I was 14, four houses near us were fire-bombed within about six months. It was scary. In our neighbourhood of mostly commission houses, people would move in and out, or the houses would stand vacant. Most tenants were unemployed and dirt poor. Many used drugs and some would go out, get petrol and just burn the places down. One family on our street had seven kids, none of whom went to school. They just roamed the street terrorising people.

I remember one evening very clearly. Mum and I hadn't realised the house across the street from us had been standing empty. We got home, had dinner and watched TV—normal stuff. At about 7.30 we started seeing light reflecting on the TV, and soon after there was a really strong smell of smoke. We didn't know what was happening, but in the back of my mind I thought, *someone's torched a house or blown up a car.* (When people in our suburb put out hard rubbish, someone would usually come along and set it alight). Six fire trucks came, the police were called and the entire street was lit up.

The next morning, in the light of day, people were still milling around and carrying on. The house was basically reduced to a pile of charcoal. The police had taped it off. Smoke still hung in the air. I think it stayed like that for about six months until the land was sold to a private investor, who built a rental property on it.

Our house was broken into a few times. When we first moved in, there was no front fence, so people would walk up and just take the furniture off the front porch. Then one night while we were sleeping they broke in and took stuff from the lounge. We only discovered the theft the next morning when we found the window open and stuff missing. Mum's jewellery probably wasn't worth much, but they took it anyway. Of course we had no insurance to replace anything. Thankfully they didn't take any substantial furniture, and we had one of those big old TVs that were hard to carry so they left that too.

Being constantly short of money caused a lot of stress for Mum, who was trying her best to provide for her family. We relied on government assistance and food stamps to ensure we could eat.

I might have been a rebel in school, but if someone threw 20 cents on the ground, I picked it up.

It wasn't fun living with the constant stress of break-ins, fires and violent people on the streets, but we just had to deal with it — it was how we lived. I watched as kids from school or the neighbourhood would be drawn into the same cycle of poverty as their parents before them, falling into the traps of drug abuse, drinking, crime and welfare dependency.

Growing up fast

My response to this experience was a bit different from most kids'. Growing up in poverty definitely made me more financially aware than most. You need money to survive. You can't buy food without it. I didn't want to end up on the dole and just continue living hand to mouth like everyone around me. I didn't want to be stuck in this shitty cycle forever. For me, how we were living was all wrong. And the thought that one day my own kids might be stuck in the same rut was even worse. So how could I fix the situation?

I started asking questions about money and property at age seven. We'd go to church, then visit one of Mum's friends in Baulkham Hills, Castle Hill, a nice area in the hill district of western Sydney. I remember they had a big flat-screen TV when they had just come out. I was blown away. They had all kinds of nice stuff in a really nice house, and the drive home from their house to ours left a deep impression on me. We'd drive from an area of big, beautiful, family-friendly homes with manicured lawns towards shabbier and shabbier houses and front yards, until we'd pass a house someone had set on fire. I remember that so clearly. And the neighbourhoods had completely different atmospheres. I knew where I wanted to be.

Visiting these people, I became obsessed with the idea of a different life. I told myself that one day I'd own one of those nice houses. I was determined that when I grew up I would make enough money so I'd never have to worry about it again.

When I was a teenager and started getting more interested in property, I realised that people who create wealth and live in nice areas usually own their home, and some owned investment properties too. At the very least they had steady jobs. No one in our family owned any property. They'd worked for 30, 40, 50 years, and still hadn't been able to lift themselves out of the same rough neighbourhood. I knew I couldn't do that. I had to do something different.

I should note that I felt more mature than other kids my age. At 12 years old I didn't feel like a child. By around age 13 or 14, I recognised that some of the financial decisions made by my parents weren't good decisions, and I knew I wanted to do something different. I felt like I was growing up really fast because I had to parent myself to some degree. I was probably a difficult teen. I don't know if I was rebellious exactly, but I thought I knew better than my mum did.

I certainly got into a lot of trouble in high school. I went to a very rough school that was infamous in western Sydney and beyond, not least for a TV documentary, *Plumpton High Babies*, that was filmed there. We had day care so girls as young as 14 or 15 could bring their babies to school. The school was the best my mum could manage, but I knew I wanted a very different future for myself and for my own kids one day. Because my family and close friends never went to university, that wasn't on my radar. I thought university or college happened only in America.

As a teenager, I would go visit my father a few times a year. He lived in the Adelaide suburb of Glenelg. When I stayed with him, he would spend a lot of time reading the paper and checking on the stocks he owned. It gave me an interest in stocks, and I did try them at one point (which I cover later). When I was 18, Dad was already 63 years old and had contracted cancer. He passed away at 71 years old, when I was 26. It was heartbreaking losing him so young. He died with no financial assets to his name, no properties, no stocks of significant value—they'd all been used up paying for his retirement and medical bills. For me, this reinforced the fact that a person could work extremely hard their entire life and still be struggling financially right to the end.

It was a hard, deeply sad lesson that only added fuel to my fire. I was determined to make money work better for me so I could create financial security and wealth over time.

My first jobs

At 14, I started working after school at KFC to help bring in some extra money, and by 16 I had switched over to McDonald's. Everybody starts somewhere, and these jobs worked well around my school hours and gave me some pocket money.

It was during my time at McDonald's that my interest in property really began to take off. A 19-year-old workmate happened to mention that he had just bought his first investment property with the help of his dad. It blew me away. How had this guy only three years older than me managed to buy a property when none of my family members or friends, or indeed anyone I knew, had managed it? If he could do it, why couldn't I? My goal of owning a home suddenly started to look achievable.

When I was 17 years old, working long shifts at McDonald's for less than $11 an hour, I would imagine where I would be financially 10 or 15 years down the track. I was certain I didn't want to keep struggling. I remember thinking, *How can I make sure I'm financially set up when I'm 30 years old? What can I do in the next few years that will put me ahead of everyone else?* As a start, I made sure I saved as much as I could. I was saving at least $200 to $250 a week out of my part-time wage of $340.

One morning I was working a very early morning shift at McDonald's with another crew member, Steve. We were doing the open shift, which means opening up the store, turning on all the equipment and getting the cooking area of the restaurant ready for preparing the breakfast food. Steve was complaining about money and how tired he was of working at Macca's—in a couple months he would have been there 10 years, and he was turning 28 years old.

I said, 'Steve, why don't you just quit here and apply for other jobs that pay more, or something you'd enjoy more?'

I still remember his reply: 'I can't quit, I don't have enough money to pay my rent, bills and car loan. And I don't have the time to look for other jobs or go to interviews because I'm always working.'

'But you have some money saved from working here for 10 years though, right? You have the nicest car!' I said, trying to make him feel better. 'You could just sell that if you needed money?' He was a car fanatic and always loved talking about his car.

'I barely have any savings. My wage goes out as fast as it comes in. I've got my car loan to pay off too! That's almost $30 000. I thought about selling the car to get rid of my loan, but I won't even get $15 000 for it now.'

'Never buy an expensive, brand-new car', he added. 'It's one of my biggest regrets. The bank charges huge interest, then after five years or so the car's not even worth half of what you paid! The car goes down in value and you can't even get your money back if you want to sell it in a few years' time.'

I could hear the regret in his voice. He knew he'd made a mistake that would cost him dearly for years.

Like Steve, many of my friends had started taking out personal loans to buy nice cars on finance. The temptation to do the same was strong. I had always wanted an old Ford Mustang and was close to dropping all my savings on the car of my dreams. Luckily, thanks to Steve's well-timed advice, common sense prevailed and I managed to resist the temptation.

But sadly, I saw lots of friends fall into the car finance trap. While they struggled to repay the loans on their quickly depreciating cars, I caught the bus, drove a bomb and continued to save money each week.

Making that choice, opting for logic over emotion, changed a lot of things for me. Had I gone and bought my dream car, I might have thought I looked cool for a while, but in the long run I would have been financially much worse off. It took a lot of discipline, but in two years I had managed to save enough for a small deposit.

I turned my focus to buying my first property. I spent many hours on the internet trawling through the real estate listings. I read and re-read the old property investment books Mum picked up for me from the op-shop (I still have them today). I got a new job as an office junior at an automotive paint shop. In this role I did the banking, calculated the daily earnings, reconciled accounts and dropped off the daily takings and receipts at the bank. Working with numbers every day was an excellent learning experience and gave me some valuable insight into the financial end of running a business.

I knew I had just enough for a deposit on an investment property, but I also knew that obtaining finance was going to be tough. I used every online mortgage calculator I came across to find out what I could borrow. Altogether I tried 11 different lenders, but my woefully low salary of $26000 ensured I was either rejected outright or offered a measly $30000 home loan. What could I buy with that? I needed to increase my income, and fast. So I took on a second job as a bartender at the local RSL, working long hours in the evenings and on weekends.

After months of setbacks and rejection, I was driving to the bank to drop off the daily takings for work when I decided it was time to go in there and speak to a lender in person. What did I have to lose? I nervously approached the counter and asked to speak with someone about getting a home loan. The teller raised her eyebrows and gave me a look. I did look pretty young. Nonetheless, she made an appointment for the following day with a mortgage lender named Kathy.

The next day I told work I would take a little longer at the bank and set off to my appointment. Kathy was awesome. Together we went through my income, expenses and overall financial situation and I felt like someone was finally taking me seriously. We spoke about the sorts of properties that I had been looking at and my expected price range. Finally, she told me what I had been waiting to hear. If the property I wanted to purchase had a rental income of over $200 a week, my borrowing capacity would be boosted to $140000. I was ecstatic. Not only had she taken the time to explain everything thoroughly in terms I could understand, but she had approved me when everyone else had said no. I walked out of that meeting with a conditional pre-approval and a spring in my step.

I couldn't believe it was finally happening—I was on track to buy my first property at just 18 years old. And with no mentor or parental help; I had done it on my own.

CHAPTER 2
Purchasing my first property

Those familiar with my story might now wish to jump to Part II and my evaluation of the different investment options. Otherwise, read on for an account of my first seven years as an investor, from owning nothing to having ten properties under my belt by the age of 25.

Due diligence

I was 18 and ready to buy my first property—I just needed to find the right one. I had already spent years studying the market on the internet, so I had a pretty firm grasp of the various suburbs of Sydney and their price ranges. It was already clear to me that even the western suburbs were going to be beyond my initial budget, so I turned to another familiar area—the Central Coast.

During the school holidays my family would occasionally go camping together, and the Central Coast of NSW was one of the only holiday destinations we could afford. It was an hour-and-a-half drive from Sydney and had a decent-sized population, as well as a seasonal influx of tourists. It seemed a lot nicer than Mount Druitt, and I thought that just maybe I could afford to buy something at the price and rental return I was looking for. I searched day and night, but although prices were lower than in Sydney, most places were still just out of my reach. Finally I came across a property listed at $145 000.

My eyes lit up as I read the description. It had two bedrooms, one bathroom, a balcony and a car space. It was only 20 minutes' drive from where we used to holiday, at The Entrance. Better still, it was rented out at $200 a week. It seemed too good to be true. Comparable properties in the same area were selling for more than $165 000. There had to be a catch. I emailed the real estate agent, Damien, and received a phone call the next day. I told him this was my first purchase and that it was all still new to me. He was very understanding and agreed to show me through the property that weekend.

Arriving at the real estate office, I was greeted by Damien and my sister, Samantha, who had agreed to come with me. We jumped into our cars and drove to the property. As we approached, it became clearer why the place was cheap. The road was full of potholes, and the 12-unit block was daubed with graffiti. Rubbish spilled out from the six commercial units on the ground floor. Samantha and I exchanged glances — it wasn't looking good.

We walked around the back and approached the door of the unit where we found a pile of junk and abandoned furniture graciously left by the former tenant. Damien was a little embarrassed. The tenants had assured him they would remove it, but they'd clearly done a runner. Despite the less-than-ideal first impression, I tried to keep an open mind.

As we entered the unit, my excitement began to creep back. Inside was not half bad! It was clean and airy, with crisp white walls and older grey carpet that still presented well. The bedrooms had built-in wardrobes and shared a breezy balcony with views of the lake. The kitchen was older-style wood grain but perfectly presentable, and there was even a second balcony off the dining area. The council rates and strata levies were reasonable. The area was quiet and in high rental demand, and I knew the unit had only been vacant for a couple of days. It was close to schools, shops and the train line. It ticked all the boxes.

I knew I had a decision to make.

I pulled Samantha aside so we could talk in private. Although the unit was nice, we were both a little concerned about the seedy state of the exterior. However, having done my due diligence, I had some facts and figures up my sleeve. I knew that the median price for units in the area was around $185 000 — a good $40 000 above the asking price. All comparable listings were over $165 000, meaning the unit was technically below market value. Finally, I could use the state of the exterior as leverage in negotiating the price down still further. Using this logic, I talked with Damien and managed to get the price down to $138 500. This was the one!

Driving back to the agent's office, I knew I had made the right choice. This place was affordable and would give me a foot on the bottom rung of the property ladder, which was exactly what I had hoped for. Half an hour later I had signed on the dotted line and engaged the agent to manage the property and begin the search for a new tenant.

I took a deep breath. I'd done it and was on my way!

My first investment property!

It's not about what it looks like — it's about the numbers, and starting the journey!

This experience set the standard for how I have purchased property ever since. By thinking rationally, keeping a cool head and conducting thorough research, I make informed decisions, which ensures I get the best possible outcomes.

Here's what the upfront costs looked like for property #1:

Purchase price	**$138 500**
10% deposit	$13 850
Lenders mortgage insurance (LMI)	$1 200
Conveyancing	$1 100
Stamp duty	$3 500
Pest and building inspection	$500
Total deposit required by bank	**$20 150**

The total mortgage repayments each week were $190, covering both principal and interest. With the unit rented out at $200 a week, it would basically be paying for itself!

When I was buying my first property, lots of terms I was unfamiliar with were thrown around by the bank and the agent, so I have included some basic definitions for the newbies out there.

Lenders mortgage insurance (LMI)

LMI is a security cost that is generally required if you are borrowing more than 80 per cent for a standard residential loan. It means if you don't have a 20 per cent deposit saved, you'll have to pay a fee to the bank because the loan is deemed to present a slightly higher risk to the bank.

In most cases, LMI can be 'capitalised' on the loan balance upon settlement, which means you don't have to come up with the money upfront — it is simply added to your home loan (and you therefore pay interest on this amount, as it forms part of the loan).

DEFINITION

Pest and building inspection

A pest and building inspection is performed by a licensed inspector who will provide a written report of the property's condition. It includes details of any significant building defects or potential issues such as rotten timber, cracks, safety hazards, the presence of asbestos or a leaking roof, and evidence of termite infestation.

It is important to identify any potential problems with the building that might surface and cost you money to repair in the future.

Principal and interest

Principal is the balance of the actual loan being paid off. *Interest* is the charge paid to the lender for the privilege of borrowing the money from them.

Mortgage loans are usually set at a default principal and interest right from the start, which means you are paying off both with each repayment you make. It is also possible to switch to an interest-only loan for a period (usually between one and five years), which will lower your repayments.

Interest-only loans offer some short-term advantages, including decreasing your initial outlay and freeing up cash flow when purchasing a property. However, borrowers sometimes run into trouble when the interest-only period ends and their repayments suddenly increase again, so it is important to use these loans as part of a thought-out strategy to ensure you don't get stung by a shortfall. You might, for example, have a plan in place to increase the rent at the end of the interest-only period.

DEFINITION

Conveyancer

Conveyancers conduct all the legal work required in a property transaction. Conveyancing plays a big part in the purchasing of property, so it is important to have at least a basic understanding of the process.

The best way to find a good conveyancer is through a referral from someone you know. It pays to do your research, read reviews and make some phone calls to ascertain whether they are credible and their fees are reasonable. You can arrange an in-person meeting or conduct the entire process remotely, from initial contact to settlement. This is particularly useful when buying property interstate.

Playing catch-up

The weeks following the exchange of contracts for my first property were both exciting and terrifying. I worried about being able to pull it all off and whether I would be able to scrape enough money together to cover all the extra fees that were popping up during the purchasing process. Not only had I just made the biggest financial decision of my life, but it was bang in the middle of the festive season. I had planned a holiday with some friends from school and I knew money was going to be tight. If I kept a cool head and remained disciplined, I could play catch-up once the property had settled.

So what does playing catch-up involve? The rule of thumb when buying properties is to have a financial buffer in place in case something goes wrong. This is standard practice and a very important strategy. It ensures you won't be caught out by un-expected fees and expenses that crop up.

Playing catch-up is a strategy I have used when purchasing a property when I don't have that buffer. This was the case with my first property. The way I see it is, if you're short of a small amount (say, $1500 for legal fees), and the property looks set to make you money upon purchase, then you do whatever it takes to pull that money together and make it happen.

It can be risky, but hear me out. The crucial piece of this strategy is that the property must be purchased *below market value*, meaning you should stand to make an immediate profit on the purchase.

So, what are some reasons a house may be being sold for lower than market value? It could be a bank repossession or the vendor may have a personal problem, such as a death in the family. There are any number of reasons. Finding such properties takes a little more time and research, but they are out there.

How can you come up with the money? The answer to this question is limited only by your imagination. You could perhaps sell something you own, borrow from a family member, put your phone bill on a payment plan to free up some cash or take out a personal loan or a cash advance on your credit card. Although borrowing money to borrow more money might sound scary, you can pay it back once you are receiving rent by living frugally for a couple of months after the sale — that is, playing catch-up.

A principle I live by that has been crucial to my journey is that sometimes you need to go through some *short-term pain* on the road to *long-term gain*. A property that is producing rental income will eventually go up in value and give you more leverage with the bank for future purchases. This is surely worth a few missed nights out, new clothes and takeaway meals.

This sort of thing isn't for everyone, and I do highly recommend having that buffer set aside if you can. If you don't have that buffer however, and if you are just starting out and are willing to put in the work, and you want it badly enough, you can usually still make it happen.

One of my favourite sayings is *fortune favours the bold*. You can do all the research, and have all the figures and the right plans in place, but taking that leap of faith will require your total confidence in yourself and your ability to pull it off. With property #1, my hard work paid off and I managed to pull together the funds in time.

Buying my first property was a huge accomplishment and the realisation of a long-held dream. All the years spent saving and researching had finally paid off, and for a moment there I thought I was done. I set about doing what most young guys do—having fun, partying and travelling. I do believe that life is there to be lived, and I enjoyed myself at the time, but looking back I believe that waiting a year and a half before buying my next property was one of the biggest mistakes I've made.

To be fair, I was still young and was proud of my achievement, but my journey had only just begun.

CHAPTER 3

My second property

Time ticked by and I changed jobs a few times, even dabbling in real estate sales. I was 19 and had always wanted to be in real estate, so I thought I'd give it a try.

I started out in a real estate office in Penrith, about 40 minutes west of Sydney's CBD. It was a blue-collar area. I didn't even own a suit and had never tied a tie in my life, so before my first day I had to go out and buy a suit that didn't look like it was from Kmart. I had no idea what I was doing. I had to borrow a car, because I was driving a disgusting 1983 Ford Laser that was full of rust. I was broke, but I had to look presentable when I showed up. In real estate how you look is extremely important.

I started learning about how a real estate office runs. That first week I knocked on doors, dropped off flyers, and put up and took down signs. Very junior stuff. I learned how agents do a comparable market analysis (CMA) and appraise properties. I called property owners to try to land their listings. I also collected leads. Anyone who has been to an open house knows that when you arrive you'll always be asked for your name, phone number and email address.

Those are leads. Agents will build up hundreds if not thousands of leads during inspections. If 40 people view a property and one person buys it, in theory the other 39 should still be in the market for a house, to buy either immediately or within six months. Those are the golden leads.

At 19, I was so shy I could barely speak, and certainly couldn't handle public speaking. I also wasn't very well educated. The truth is, I hated that job the entire time I was doing it. I loved property, so I thought I'd love working in the industry, but I didn't like this kind of involvement at all. I worked very hard, six days a week, but it felt like I was *always* working but not earning anything for those extra hours. I felt awkward and uncomfortable trying to sell. Looking back, I realise I just wasn't ready to communicate directly with the public. After a month I knew it wasn't for me.

Next I got a job with an IT company in the city. It was very basic admin and data entry, but it worked for me. Every day I caught the train from western Sydney to north Sydney. The trip took an hour and a half and carried me from one of the roughest areas in Sydney to one of the nicest parts of the city. Each morning I went from being surrounded by poverty and despair to working in a really fancy part of Sydney among well-educated people who had good jobs, wore smart clothes and drove nice cars. It felt like I was passing from one world to another, and it was a big shock at the time.

I did that for a year and a half, and I liked it. It was a standard admin job. No sales, no more money for working harder and nothing to do with property, but it suited me at the time.

My $50000 salary wasn't going too far though, especially with my partying lifestyle. After a few too many late nights and money down the drain, I started to sober up when I came across other young investors with four or more properties under their belt.

This brought out my competitive side. I knew I needed to knuckle down. Why should I stop at one?

Getting real

While others were messing around on Facebook I started poring over realestate.com. I used my time on the train to read Robert Kiyosaki's *Rich Dad, Poor Dad* and property investment books. Mum was on a pension, but she'd buy $1 books from the Salvos for me: 'Here's a property book you might like'. I read voraciously. It was inspirational stuff. Thanks to all those books and others, my mindset really started to change. And travelling every day from our rough area to this nice area had me thinking, *How do I get from here to there?* Literally.

I arranged a meeting with the lending manager at the closest bank to talk over my options. I had $10000 in savings, and my property had recently been valued at a very conservative $150000. At the time, I didn't understand the difference between a full evaluation and a drive-by evaluation — a crucial distinction I cover in chapter 10. I was offered the chance to use the equity in my first property to purchase a second, using my savings to cover the other costs. With my current loan sitting at $120000, I could have two loans sitting at 90 per cent LVR (loan-to-value ratio). Here's how those figures stacked up:

Value of property	$150000
90% (LVR) of value	$135000
Balance of loan	$120000
Equity available	$15000
Savings	$10000
Deposit power	**$25000**

> **DEFINITION**
>
> ### *Loan-to-value ratio (LVR)*
>
> Loan-to-value ratio is a risk assessment tool used by lenders. It is calculated by dividing the required mortgage amount by the bank's appraised value of the property, expressed as a percentage. The higher your deposit, the lower your loan-to-value ratio. Generally, you will receive better loan terms if your LVR is below 80 per cent.

> **DEFINITION**
>
> ### *Equity*
>
> Essentially, equity refers to the portion of your property's value that is not owned by the mortgage company. The more you pay down the mortgage, the greater your equity and the higher the value of the property. You can access your equity via a loan or a line of credit.

The bank determined that I had a borrowing capacity of $200 000, but because of my low deposit power ($25 000), I would be able to borrow only another $140 000. Not much, but good enough for me!

The search

With the finance sorted, I began the search for property #2 in earnest. From the start, my strategy had been to stick to major capital cities, but it was clear that Sydney remained unaffordable, so I broadened my search to include properties under $200 000 across Australia. I travelled to inspections all over regional New South Wales and found that the asking prices in these far-flung locations were still possible to find in metro areas.

I figured that in the future, properties within a reasonable commuting distance from a CBD would be more desirable to a growing population experiencing increasing urban sprawl and the high demand for housing, not to mention better job prospects and a global trend towards urbanisation.

I still visited my dad in Adelaide every few months, and during these visits I noticed that housing prices in the city were much lower than those in Sydney, and the yields also tended to be much higher.

Yield

The yield of a property is the annual return you expect on your investment. It is calculated by expressing a year's rental income as a percentage of how much the property cost. The table below uses property #1 as an example.

DEFINITION

The yield of property #1 is calculated as follows:

Cost		$138 500
Rent	($200/week x 52)	$10 400
Yield	([10 400 ÷ 138 500] × 100)	7.50%

Real estate agents will commonly tell you that a return of 3 to 4 per cent is good. At this rate, however, the property is likely losing money from a cash flow perspective.

By now I had some familiarity with Adelaide, so I began to target properties within a 30-minute drive of the CBD. My goal was to find another property for less than $140 000 that was renting out at $200 per week. I checked vacancy rates and rental prices online.

I also called up local agents to gather as much information on the different suburbs as possible and explained the sort of place I was looking for.

Eventually I focused my search on a few suburbs where prices were substantially lower than the median but average yields were above 7 per cent. These parts of Adelaide reminded me of where I had grown up in Sydney, but were much more affordable. On one of my visits I attended seven open homes and four drive-pasts before receiving a phone call from an agent I had connected with while conducting my research. He had found a property that was being repossessed (also known as a *mortgagee in possession*) and was due to be listed on the market the following week. The bank was asking $138 000, and I could inspect it that very day.

Turning up to the inspection, I was immediately impressed. It was a neat and tidy three-bedroom house, with a recently renovated kitchen and bathroom. It had timber floors and newly built verandahs at the front and the back of the house. It was on a large block of 640 square metres (I mentally flagged it for possible subdivision in the future). It was one of the best-looking and most well-presented houses on the street; comparable properties in worse condition were selling for at least $150 000. A quick internet search revealed that the property had sold six years earlier for $144 000. The bank was obviously seeking a quick and easy sale to recoup their capital, and I was only too happy to oblige. I negotiated with the agent and managed to get the price down to $130 000, which was 10 to 15 per cent below market value, and signed the contract then and there.

Table 3.1 shows how the figures stacked up.

Table 3.1: cash flow figures for property #2

Estimated expenses	Weekly ($)	Monthly ($)	Annually ($)
Council rates	23.08	100.00	1200.00
Strata fees, inc. building insurance	–	–	–
Water rates	23.08	100.00	1200.00
Building insurance	7.69	33.33	400.00
Management fees	17.31	75.00	900.00
Mortgage repayments	96.15	416.67	5000.00
Landlord insurance	5.77	25.00	300.00
Estimated totals	**173.08**	**750.00**	**9000.00**
Income comparables			
Lower rent	220.00	953.33	11440.00
Higher rent	240.00	1040.00	12480.00
Estimated cash flow before tax			
Lower rent	46.92	203.33	2440.00
Higher rent	66.92	290.00	3480.00

It took several weeks but finally the agent got back to me on behalf of the bank, which had accepted the offer, and the contracts were exchanged. All I had to do was organise a pest and building inspection and arrange for a solicitor to do the conveyancing.

Property #2 was house and land in Adelaide

I was now two properties in and loving it!

Growth vs cash flow

After buying my second investment property, I knew I wanted more. I decided that my big, hairy, audacious goal would be to buy ten properties by the time I was 25. That would be incredible! I continued working, socialising a little on weekends, being frugal and saving as much as I could. I also kept up my research. I read more books, watched hundreds of hours on YouTube and networked with other like-minded investors. I researched properties listed for sale online, sales and rental history, and market cycles. I got to know a number of geographic areas within Australia, and found a few key suburbs in Queensland, New South Wales, Victoria and South Australia on which to focus my search.

I found that properties within 45 minutes of the CBD in New South Wales and Victoria were selling for $400 000 to $600 000, yet producing rent of $300 to $400 a week. This equates to a yield of only 4 or 5 per cent. This meant they were negatively geared and technically losing money.

Negative gearing

Lots of people invest in property for the tax breaks and depreciation benefits. There are some advantages to this strategy, but it's not one I necessarily recommend.

Negative gearing

Negative gearing is a practice whereby an investor borrows money to acquire an income-producing investment property and expects the gross income generated by the investment to be less than the cost of owning and managing the investment. These costs include depreciation and interest charged on the loan, but not capital repayments. The losses are then used as tax breaks. Essentially, you are losing money in order to claim a portion of it back.

DEFINITION

Negative gearing arrangements offer a form of financial leverage. Investors expect that the tax benefits (if any) and the capital gain on the investment (when it is eventually disposed of) will exceed the accumulated losses of holding the investment. It is a *growth* strategy.

A major downside of this practice is that you are relying on a long-term payoff to offset your short-term losses. However, these losses can make a big dent in your present cash flow, particularly if you are a young, first-time investor or on a lower income. Furthermore, if the time comes when you are no longer working and paying tax to claim these deductions, you will still have to come up with the shortfall, which can easily add up to $10000 per annum per property (and in many cases, much more).

For me, it makes more sense to build your portfolio from a *cash flow positive* or *cash flow neutral* position. I believe it's okay to have a few negatively geared properties, based perhaps on their instant equity position or future growth potential, but these should be balanced with cash flow positive properties to help lighten the burden. It is also important to have a balancing strategy in place in case something goes wrong, such as an extended period of vacancy for the property.

Table 3.2 breaks down the cash flow position of my second property.

Table 3.2: calculations for property #2

Expenses	Weekly ($)	Monthly ($)	Annually ($)
Council rates	23.08	100.00	1200.00
Strata fees	–	–	–
Water rates	23.08	100.00	1200.00
Building insurance	17.31	75.00	900.00
Management fees	35.38	153.33	1840.00
Mortgage repayments	403.85	1750.00	21000.00
Landlord insurance	5.77	25.00	300.00
Estimated totals	**508.46**	**2203.33**	**26440.00**
Income cash flow			
Lower rent	350.00	1516.67	18200.00
Higher rent	380.00	1646.67	19760.00
Estimated cash flow before tax consideration			
Lower rent	-158.46	-686.67	-8240.00
Higher rent	-128.46	-556.67	-6680.00

There's a common argument that growing value is more important than negative cash flow. A growth property at $400000 may increase in value by 10 per cent each year (an equity gain of $40000) while losing only $10000 per annum in negative cash flow. This sounds good on paper, but it depends on the property increasing in value by 10 per cent, and this cannot be guaranteed. When coupled with the uncertainty of being able to absorb the negative cash flow when faced with financial difficulties, this is not an option for everyone.

CHAPTER 4
The buying spree

I was now 23 years old, still working full time and getting paid a pittance. I kept struggling and kept saving. I had my first two properties revalued and managed to release some equity. Coupled with my savings, I scraped together enough to keep the ball rolling and start searching for property #3.

To diversify my portfolio I decided to shift my focus to Queensland. I figured it would be smart not to hold all my eggs in one basket, and Queensland was beginning to see some big investment in infrastructure. My research showed that the market had been dormant since the 2008 Global Financial Crisis, when prices took a hit. Despite this, rents appeared to have stayed roughly the same, as people still needed a place to live.

Property #3

I came across a small one-bedroom residential unit just 30 minutes from the Brisbane CBD, listed for $120 000 and renting at $220 a week. The sales history of other units in the same building showed that identical units had sold for more than \$160 000 in 2009, before the market slowed down. I also saw that one had sold recently for \$135 000.

The online advertisement for the property—obviously created by a second-rate agency—was very brief, with no photographs. It was clear the agent didn't have much interest in pushing the property. I've since found that it's common for second-rate agencies to post inaccurate or incomplete advertisements, as well as showing the most variance in terms of market appraisals. Properties are often listed too low or high. Many people fail to see the opportunity in this. I've discovered it's usually worth investigating such listings.

It's also important to note that this property had an internal size of only 38 square metres. The general rule of thumb is that if a unit or townhouse has a floor space of less than 40 square metres and is under strata or body corporate, banks will require a deposit of at least 20 per cent. Luckily, as the unit was so cheap, it wasn't going to be too difficult for me, but it's something to keep in mind when you're looking to buy a small place.

I knew a bargain when I saw it and I settled the property a month later. It has been fully tenanted ever since. The best part? After bumping up the rent to \$240 a week, I was left with a yield of a whopping *11 per cent*. I now had \$1040 in rental income coming into my account each month, with mortgage repayments of just \$330 and expenses such as rates, strata levies and insurance totalling \$315. This left me with \$308+ per month in my pocket, or an annual pay rise of \$3600.

Table 4.1 shows how the numbers stacked up.

Table 4.1: calculations for property #3

Estimated expenses	Weekly ($)	Monthly ($)	Annually ($)
Council rates	28.85	125.00	1500.00
Strata fees inc. building insurance	32.69	141.67	1700.00
Water rates	21.15	91.67	1100.00
Building insurance	–	–	–
Management fees	16.35	70.83	850.00
Mortgage repayments (current rate)	61.54	266.67	3200.00
Landlord insurance	6.15	26.67	320.00
Estimated totals	**166.73**	**722.50**	**8670.00**
Income comparables			
Lower rent	240.00	1040.00	12480.00
Higher rent	270.00	1170.00	14040.00
Estimated cash flow before tax			
Lower rent	73.27	317.50	3810.00
Higher rent	103.27	447.50	5370.00

Oh what a feeling! – property #3

Property #4

Just two weeks after settling property #3, I came across another Queensland property that was too good to pass up. Located in an excellent position on the Gold Coast, this one-bedroom unit was 500 metres from a major shopping centre and within walking distance of the beach. It was fully renovated and had a rental appraisal of $295 a week. I managed to secure the property for $169 000, giving me a yield of 9 per cent.

I negotiated a 45-day settlement with a two-week pest, building and finance clause to give myself time to build up a deposit, as my savings were depleted from my last purchase. I got a conditional approval on finance subject to the funds being in my account by the finance clause date, in 21 days' time.

I needed to pull together $18 000 fast. First I got to work selling things from my room, like clothes, shoes and other possessions. This got me the first $3000. I took on extra shifts at a casual job for another $1000. With $14 000 to go, I started to worry. I took a $2000 cash advance from a credit card I had stashed away, then I sold my car, which brought in just enough money to get the deal done.

Four months later I was sure I'd made the right choice. I had property #3 valued, which came back higher than expected, releasing $28 000 worth of equity. I bought a much cheaper car to get around in. By making some big short-term sacrifices, I had managed to secure a great deal on property #4, which instantly created another $30 000 in equity. If I had relied on saving up for the total deposit, it would have taken me ten months or so, and that property would have been long gone.

Again, sometimes you just need to take that leap of faith.

Table 4.2 shows how the numbers stacked up.

Table 4.2: calculations for property #4

Estimated expenses	Weekly ($)	Monthly ($)	Annually ($)
Council rates	26.92	116.67	1400.00
Strata fees inc. building insurance	38.46	166.67	2000.00
Water rates	25.00	108.33	1300.00
Building insurance	–	–	–
Management fees	21.15	91.67	1100.00
Mortgage repayments (current interest rate)	86.54	375.00	4500.00
Landlord insurance	6.73	29.17	350.00
Estimated totals	**204.81**	**887.50**	**10650.00**
Income comparables			
Lower rent	290.00	1256.67	15080.00
Higher rent	335.00	1451.67	17420.00
Estimated positive cash flow before tax			
Lower rent	85.19	369.17	4430.00
Higher rent	130.19	564.17	6770.00

Property #4, by the skin of my teeth!

The side hustle

It was clear to me that I would have to increase my income if I wanted to speed up the process of building my portfolio. The more I made, the faster I could save up deposits and the higher my borrowing capacity would be.

On top of my 40-hour office job, I started tending bar again, working 25 to 35 hours a week on evenings and weekends. I won't lie, it was tough sometimes. But I kept reminding myself: a little short-term pain for a lot of long-term gain. This was my *why*. I knew I didn't want to be working this much when I had a family one day, so I had to do it now, while I was completely independent.

It's a strategy I highly recommend: if you are serious about investing, do whatever you can to boost your income, particularly when you're young. Take on an extra job, or ask for a raise. Learn a value-producing skill, buy and sell second-hand goods, sell things at a market... whatever! It all adds up. A side hustle is a great way to spend your time productively and help set you up so you won't have to work so hard in future.

Property #5

Taking on the second job allowed me to build up my savings to prepare for property #5. I saved almost every cent I made, cutting back even further on unnecessary expenses.

I decided on some key target markets and began to research these areas actively. I forged relationships with local real estate agents and emphasised my interest in off-market opportunities. Eventually I received a phone call from an agent in South Australia. He had found a three-bedroom house on a 600-square-metre block in Adelaide, close to property #2. I knew that comparable properties were selling for $150 000 plus, but the agent was asking $130 000. The owner was desperate to sell due to financial issues. It hadn't even officially hit the market, but the agent knew it was exactly the sort of thing I was looking for and got in touch straightaway.

I did some research online and discovered that the property next door had recently sold for $155 000. I also noticed that it was currently under-rented at $190 per week, when comparable properties were going for $240. It was another no-brainer. I managed to negotiate a price of $125 000 and bought it sight unseen.

Boosting the rent to the market rate gave this property a yield of 9.1 per cent. In addition, having purchased it at such a good price, I knew I could get it revalued in six to eight months' time and be able to retrieve the entire $30 000 that I had put into it back in equity. Being a positively geared property, after all expenses I was left with an annual pay rise of over $5000.

Table 4.3 (overleaf) shows how the numbers stacked up.

Property #5 was a house on a huge block of land within 30 minutes of Adelaide's CBD

Table 4.3: calculations for property #5

Estimated expenses	Weekly ($)	Monthly ($)	Annually ($)
Council rates	21.15	91.67	1100.00
Strata fees inc. building insurance	–	–	–
Water rates	15.38	66.67	800.00
Building insurance	9.62	41.67	500.00
Management fees	19.23	83.33	1000.00
Mortgage repayments (current interest rate)	63.46	275.00	3300.00
Landlord insurance	6.73	29.17	350.00
Estimated totals	**135.58**	**587.50**	**7050.00**
Income comparables			
Lower rent	240.00	1040.00	12480.00
Higher rent	280.00	1213.33	14560.00
Estimated positive cash flow before tax			
Lower rent	104.42	452.50	5430.00
Higher rent	144.42	625.83	7510.00

The struggle for #6

Property #5 was settled and I was on a roll. I had a few options when it came to buying property #6. I could save the money for the deposit, which could take anywhere from ten to 14 months, or release equity from properties #1 and #2. The equity in property #2 had never been released, so I knew that quite a bit would have accumulated by now. I decided to use a mix of savings and equity. I was still working long hours at my two jobs and saving like a madman.

This time I decided to use a broker to obtain finance. It was one of the few times I put faith and confidence in the wrong person. The broker had approached several banks seeking valuations. When I finally got them back, they looked great. I figured that combined with my excellent record and healthy credit rating, obtaining finance was going to be a breeze. Unfortunately, the broker bore some bad news. My loan had been refused due to the number of credit enquiries on my file.

I was furious, but learned a valuable lesson on the importance of structuring your purchases and timing your credit enquiries. The bank and the broker recommended that I wait six months, and in the meantime try to mitigate the decision with the credit department. This would involve meeting with bank representatives and explaining the situation to have the decision overruled manually. It would take months.

I went to four different banks and spoke to a bunch of brokers, trying to find a way around it, but none of them were able to help. I spoke to three different mortgage lenders at the same bank before finding one I felt I could trust and build a relationship with. Given the tedious nature of refinancing and the complexity involved with managing the financials of multiple properties, it is very important to work with people you trust.

After six months' stagnation, I finally managed to get it sorted. I refinanced three property loans, keeping them separate rather than cross-collateralised. I was also able to release equity from three of my five properties. This gave me a deposit for property #6 and enough left over to pay off outstanding debt and significantly improve my cash flow.

Cross-collateralisation

Cross-collateralisation means using more than one property to secure a loan. It can be beneficial for investors, as you don't need to use as much cash for a deposit, but it can also throw the balance of power in favour of the bank and limit your choices if you want to sell, refinance or access equity in future.

I focused again on south-east Queensland and soon came across a two-bedroom property not far from Brisbane that initially had been listed at $199000, then dropped to $189000, then again to $179000. Once again I did my research. I found that comparable units, even identical units in the same block, were selling for much more. After speaking with the agent I learned that the owner was retiring and needed to get the property sold and settled this side of the financial year end.

With the promise of a quick settlement and the assurance that I would sign the contract within the hour, I negotiated a final price of $165000. The unit was rented at $240 per week, but my research showed that others were going for as much as $285. If I increased the rent to reflect the market, the property would have a return of 8.9 per cent. Having purchased it significantly below market value, I knew I would be able to have it revalued for anywhere between $185000 and $200000, and if I put down a 20 per cent deposit, I could potentially release 90 per cent of the deposit in six to eight months' time. That 20 per cent deposit and all associated fees and costs totalled $38000. I settled my sixth investment property 32 days later.

Table 4.4 shows how the numbers stacked up.

Table 4.4: calculations for property #6

Estimated expenses	Weekly ($)	Monthly ($)	Annually ($)
Council rates	30.77	133.33	1600.00
Strata fees inc. building insurance	40.38	175.00	2100.00
Water rates	21.15	91.67	1100.00
Building insurance	–	–	–
Management fees	17.31	75.00	900.00
Mortgage repayments (current interest rate)	78.85	341.67	4100.00
Landlord insurance	6.73	29.17	350.00
Estimated totals	**195.19**	**845.83**	**10150.00**
Income comparables			
Lower rent	285.00	1235.00	14820.00
Higher rent	300.00	1300.00	15600.00
Estimated cash flow before tax			
Lower rent	89.81	389.17	4670.00
Higher rent	104.81	454.17	5450.00

Number six at last

CHAPTER 5
Achieving my property dreams

According to the Australian Taxation Office, 72.8 per cent of individuals who own an investment property own just one, 18 per cent own two, and just 0.9 per cent of individuals own six or more.

Reaching #6 was a huge milestone for me, particularly as I had managed to do it at only 24 years of age. I had achieved something many people only dream of doing. There was (and still is) lots of talk in the media about housing affordability crises in Sydney and Melbourne, and the struggles many millennials face when it comes to entering the property market. When word started to get out that some poor kid from Mount Druitt had bucked the trend and managed to buy not one but six properties, I started to attract media attention.

In the space of two months I had two television appearances, an article in the *Sydney Morning Herald* and a feature and video on the Domain website. This exposure drummed up a lot of interest. People recognised me in the street, added me on social media and slid into my DMs both to congratulate me and to ask for advice.

Everyone was keen to learn how I'd managed it. It was all a bit overwhelming, but I knew I had something to be proud of and an interesting story to share.

Career and lifestyle choices

An increasingly obvious truth that was looming over the dream of building my portfolio was that my low income was hurting my borrowing capacity. Something had to give. If I wanted to keep up this level of momentum and achieve my vision, I needed more money coming in.

I made the decision to change industries entirely and took a job in sales that saw me selling industrial tools for an annual income of $80 000 plus. Coupled with my bartending job, my annual income now topped $100 000, which was a significant boost. The extra money coming in allowed me to take a six-week holiday in Europe with my girlfriend. It was the first time I'd travelled overseas as an adult, and it felt incredible.

A property portfolio that was profitable and self-sustaining meant I didn't have to worry about taking six weeks off work. The properties were taking care of themselves and producing a steady income while I went off and had the time of my life. Having spent the last few years working so hard in two different jobs, it was totally liberating to have that time to just relax and unwind. I'll admit, though, that even while overseas I tried to close a deal on another place, which I just missed out on. It's hard to resist a bargain!

We had a wonderful trip. I proposed to Francesca on a beach in Spain at sunset. Coming home, I felt refreshed, relaxed and inspired to go even harder than before. I vowed to build my portfolio to the point where I could go travelling for months, years or the rest of my life if I chose to. I set my sights on achieving the total financial freedom offered by passive income, and I was determined to make it happen.

Property #7

So I got straight back into it. Two jobs, 80-hour weeks, pedal to the metal. I followed the emerging property markets around Brisbane religiously, seeking out the next deal that would get me closer to my goals. I networked with many local agents. First I'd call about properties I'd seen online. I'd introduce myself, tell them the criteria for the properties I was targeting and my price range, then ask them to give me a call when something suitable came up.

Finally an agent contacted me with a property. It was going on the market the following week, and the owner was in financial difficulties and desperate to sell. It was a modern, two-bedroom townhouse just 30 minutes from the Brisbane CBD, renting out at $270 per week. Recent sales in the complex were sitting around $185 000, and my research showed they had previously been fetching $230 000. I negotiated a price of $158 000 and signed the contract, but I was going to struggle to come up with that deposit so fast. I knew the property had potential, and having bought it at such a great price I knew it would be a good investment that offered an instant equity gain. It would be hard to secure finance for the property, but I decided I simply wouldn't take no for an answer.

My savings had been depleted by my trip overseas. I reviewed my portfolio and decided that my fourth property, which I had purchased nine months earlier, would have risen in price since the purchase. As I bought it below market value, I knew there should be enough equity there to make it happen. I spoke with one of my more trusted bank managers to get the property valued and the finance process moving. After a few weeks of hitting brick walls and some back and forth between the bank and myself, I finally managed to get the loan. It came at a cost, though, as I had to cross-collateralise the property with my fourth. This is something I try to avoid, but in this case there was no other way. With the finance secured and the property settled, I was free to keep working and saving my money for the next deposit.

Table 5.1 shows how the numbers stacked up.

Table 5.1: estimated expenses for property #7

Estimated expenses	Weekly ($)	Monthly ($)	Annually ($)
Council rates	26.92	116.67	1400.00
Strata fees inc. building insurance	42.31	183.33	2200.00
Water rates	19.23	83.33	1000.00
Building insurance	–	–	–
Management fees	20.19	87.50	1050.00
Mortgage repayments (current interest rate)	98.08	425.00	5100.00
Landlord insurance	6.73	29.17	350.00
Estimated totals	**213.46**	**925.00**	**11100.00**
Income comparables			
Lower rent	280.00	1213.33	14560.00
Higher rent	320.00	1386.67	16640.00
Estimated cash flow before tax			
Lower rent	66.54	288.33	3460.00
Higher rent	106.54	461.67	5540.00

Inspecting property #7. I was 23 years old.

Property #8

I spent the next five months working really long hours and saving as much of my income as I could. It took a lot of self-control, but I knew this temporary sacrifice meant I could live an easier life in the future.

For property #8 I decided to focus again on the Gold Coast. There continued to be a flurry of investment and infrastructure projects occurring there, and the region was experiencing high population growth and a subsequent demand for housing. I had seen price rises of 20 per cent for some units close to where I had purchased my fourth property.

As I was searching online one night I came across a one-bedroom unit. Experience had taught me that many agents tended to upload new listings to the internet at night, so it's an excellent time to get a first look of the latest offerings. It was listed for $200 000. A quick search showed that similar properties had recently sold for between $220 000 and $240 000.

The next morning I negotiated a price of $180 000.

Below is a breakdown of the numbers for the deal for property #8:

Purchase price	**$180 000**
10% Deposit	$18 000
LMI	$3 000
Conveyancing	$1 500
Stamp duty	$5 000
Pest and building inspection	$500
Cost outlay	$28 000
Loan amount	**$162 000**

I organised a valuation with another bank, which came back at $230 000. This meant I had managed to turn my initial cost outlay of $28 000 into $50 000 with a net capital gain (on paper). Checking over the calculations, I realised that this was the same as an entire year's salary at one of my old jobs. I used to travel three hours a day, work eight to ten hours and do this 52 weeks of the year to earn what I had just made in a couple of hours!

Table 5.2 shows how the numbers stacked up.

Table 5.2: calculations for property #8

Estimated expenses	Weekly ($)	Monthly ($)	Annually ($)
Council rates	38.46	166.67	2000.00
Strata fees inc. building insurance	48.08	208.33	2500.00
Water rates	19.23	83.33	1000.00
Building insurance	–	–	–
Management fees	17.31	75.00	900.00
Mortgage repayments (current interest rate)	55.77	241.67	2900.00
Landlord insurance	5.96	25.83	310.00
Estimated totals	**184.81**	**800.83**	**9610.00**
Income comparables			
Lower rent	260.00	1126.67	13520.00
Higher rent	270.00	1170.00	14040.00
Estimated cash flow before tax			
Lower rent	75.19	325.83	3910.00
Higher rent	85.19	369.17	4430.00

By this time I knew this was exactly what I wanted to do for the rest of my life. I also started to realise that I was developing the tools and confidence to be able to help others do the same.

Property #8, a great property in the heart of the Gold Coast

Property #9

I now owned properties across three different states with very different markets. I wanted to continue to diversify my portfolio using my fundamental formula of buying under-market properties in metro areas that were cash-flow positive from day one. Through my research, I discovered some affordable properties close to the CBD in Cairns that were achieving yields between 8 and 12 per cent. Reviewing the previous 20 years of property growth cycles, I recognised similar trends and patterns to what had been happening in Brisbane. Both markets had risen steeply between 2003 and 2008, then taken a fall after the GFC.

In Cairns, two-bedroom townhouses that sold for $80 000 in 2002 were fetching anywhere from $100 000 to $140 000 by the end of 2008. Fast forward to now, and the same properties were still fetching between $100 000 and $140 000. This meant the market had been mostly stagnant for almost nine years, with some outliers in the inner suburbs fluctuating by 10 per cent. Cairns also had low vacancy rates, meaning there was a strong demand for rental properties.

Over the following months I monitored the market and found the best value for money was in townhouses, which also made applying for finance easier, as they were over the 40 square metre threshold and therefore not subject to the 20 per cent deposit rule.

I eventually found a two-bedroom townhouse just 10 minutes from the Cairns CBD. It was neat and tidy, and fitted all my criteria. Properties in the same complex were selling for between $130000 and $140000. The owners of this one, however, were going through a messy divorce and needed a quick sale. The property was rented out to long-term tenants who wanted to stay on. I managed to negotiate a price of $106000, and with the rent fetching $240 a week, I had a yield of 9.8 per cent. Furthermore, I saw a number of comparable properties being rented at $240 per week, which gave me an option to improve on that yield when the tenants' lease came up for renewal.

Table 5.3 (overleaf) shows how the numbers stacked up.

Nine down, one to go!

Table 5.3: calculations for property #9

Estimated expenses	Weekly ($)	Monthly ($)	Annually ($)
Council rates	21.15	91.67	1100.00
Strata fees inc. building insurance	–	–	–
Water rates	15.38	66.67	800.00
Building insurance	11.54	50.00	600.00
Management fees	19.23	83.33	1000.00
Mortgage repayments (current interest rate)	59.62	258.33	3100.00
Landlord insurance	865.00	37.50	450.00
Estimated totals	**135.58**	**587.50**	**7050.00**
Income comparables			
Lower rent	240.00	1040.00	12480.00
Higher rent	280.00	1213.33	14560.00
Estimated cash flow before tax			
Lower rent	104.42	452.50	5430.00
Higher rent	144.42	625.83	7510.00

Mentoring others

My story was continuing to spread. The more properties I bought, the more interested people were in how I had managed to do it. I received a steady stream of emails and messages on social media from complete strangers who wanted to connect with me and ask for advice. I always took the time to respond and found that I was really enjoying helping and working with people who were just as passionate about achieving financial security as I was. Most of them were hardworking people who did not know where to start and were looking for tips and tricks to help them get their foot in the door.

I was only too happy to oblige, as I remembered how scary and unattainable it had seemed when I was still working and saving towards my first investment, and how badly I wished I had a mentor to offer me guidance at the time. I started to realise that helping others to build successful property portfolios could develop into a business venture that utilised all the knowledge and experience I had been accumulating on this journey.

Property #10

Meanwhile I continued working and saving, and by the middle of 2017 I was ready for property #10. My strategy remained unchanged. I wanted somewhere in the metro area with a low entry price and high rental yield that could be purchased at below market value.

My previous four properties had all been in Queensland, so I decided to head back to Adelaide, which still had properties with high yields and low vacancy rates. As luck would have it, I received a phone call from a local agent with whom I had built a strong rapport some months earlier. They had a two-bedroom house on a 500-square-metre block just 30 minutes from the Adelaide CBD. I negotiated another bargain price of just $110000 and it settled a month later.

I had reached my goal of owning 10 properties by the age of 25, and it felt incredible. The road had not been easy, but I had persevered through the tough times, pushed myself, until I achieved my dream.

Table 5.4 (overleaf) shows how the numbers stacked up.

Table 5.4: calculations for property #10

Estimated expenses	Weekly ($)	Monthly ($)	Annually ($)
Council rates	21.15	91.67	1100.00
Strata fees inc. building insurance	–	–	–
Water rates	15.38	66.67	800.00
Building insurance	11.54	50.00	600.00
Management fees	19.23	83.33	1000.00
Mortgage repayments (current interest rate)	59.62	258.33	3100.00
Landlord insurance	8.65	37.50	450.00
Estimated totals	**135.58**	**58750**	**7050.00**
Income comparables			
Lower rent	240.00	1040.00	12480.00
Higher rent	280.00	1213.33	14560.00
Estimated cash flow before tax			
Lower rent	104.42	452.50	5430.00
Higher rent	144.42	625.83	7510.00

Once I hit this target my story was picked up by the media again. I received requests to be interviewed and featured on a number of news and current affairs programs across the country. I was stoked to have the opportunity to share my story and was soon overwhelmed with people seeking advice on getting into the property market. I started arranging phone meetings with people who wanted to pick my brain, ask my opinion and discuss finance and investment strategies. I found myself easing into this role of educator and guide, and loving the conversation and challenge of the role I found myself in.

Number 10 is another small house on a huge block of land.

Founding Dilleen Property

There was clearly a demand for property investment advice, and I was perfectly positioned to provide it. At the time, the industry was full of companies led and staffed by people with very little property investing experience. Their primary objective was to sell properties to clients, take their commission and be on their way. Some of the founders of these companies owned only a couple of properties themselves while making grand promises to their customers about building portfolios of five to ten properties, without the experience to back them up. The frustrating thing was that so many people believed them and were paying good money to do business with them. Some of these people had got in touch with me and shared how they found themselves with properties that were highly negatively geared or bought overpriced off the plan. They were stuck with 'investment' properties that were sucking them dry and preventing them from buying any more.

After doling out advice in my spare time to various people via email and by phone, I realised I could be doing more good by quitting my job and focusing all my energy on helping others to invest in property. I loved what I was doing and had learned so much along the way. Why not use everything I had learned to help other people achieve their dreams?

So I founded Dilleen Property, and I've never looked back.

Dilleen Property allows me to take the time to work one-on-one with my clients. I love the opportunity to learn about their *why*, their goals and their current situation, then devise strategies that will help them and their families to secure their financial future. I get the same rush when I secure a great deal for my clients as when I do so for myself. I'm doing a job I love and helping people at the same time. What more could I ask for?

PART II

INVESTMENT STRATEGIES

There are many approaches to investing money in property for the purpose of achieving a good return. At the beginning of my journey I trawled through a massive amount of (often conflicting) information related to different strategies. I explored multiple avenues but quickly chose a specific strategy, and I stayed with it, as I believe it is both the best and the most accessible method. But don't take my word for it. Let's dive into the different options, and review some of the pros and cons. Then you can decide for yourself.

If you are keen to jump straight into the different strategies and tactics I have personally used to grow my multimillion-dollar property empire, you may choose to jump to chapter 8. I hope it excites you and lights the fire in your belly half as much as it did in mine!

CHAPTER 6
Property vs stocks

I bought some stocks when I was 18 years old, even before I bought my first investment property. My dad's interest in the stock market persuaded me to consider them as an investment vehicle. So I sunk $500 in stocks, which fell to zero in a matter of months. Losing that $500 was painful. I decided that at that stage in my life property investment was a safer option, because a property will always be worth something—it can never drop to zero value, as my stocks did. I also liked that with property you get land, and there isn't any more land being created, so it's a finite resource! Furthermore, an investment property draws a rental income, and I knew I could use that leverage to my advantage, so I decided to focus on property investing and maybe review stocks sometime in the future.

Deciding whether to invest in real estate or in stocks is a personal choice that will depend on your financial situation, goals and tolerance of risk. When you buy stocks, you're buying a tiny piece of a company. You make money as the value of the company's stock increases, and through dividend payments, which you can reinvest to grow your investment.

For me, property is a much safer investment. What I especially like about property is you can use leverage to leapfrog forward: you can put down only 10 per cent of your capital and borrow the other 90 per cent from the bank or another lender. So you may put down just $40000 but you control a $400000 asset.

There are many ways of winning with property. Owning investment properties (if done in the right way) can provide you with cash flow through passive income (your income is greater than your expenses, and you net the difference). Not all stocks pay dividends (though most companies on the ASX 200 do), but your passive income from stocks is usually only 5 to 10 per cent of the amount you've put in. So whereas you might put $40000 down, own an asset worth $400000 and make money (if it's cash flow positive) from day one, with stocks you would need to invest $1 million to create $50000 to $100000 a year in passive income.

Also, property values usually continue to rise (in Australia they have done so for decades), so while you're collecting your passive income, the value of your asset is appreciating too. Furthermore, real estate can be leveraged in a way that stocks can't: when a property increases in value, you can use that equity as the deposit for your next property.

In my opinion, the stock market can be more volatile than the property market, as we saw during the COVID-19 pandemic, when the stock market plummeted! Property is a physical asset that also meets a social need. People will always need a place to live. We will always need shelter for ourselves and our families. On top of that, the population is always going to be growing. Look at the world population 10, 20 and 50 years ago compared with now. As the population grows, more people will need a place to live. So to me it's a no-brainer that the best investment on earth is earth itself—land.

Figure 6.1 shows how a $90 000 investment in superannuation will grow over 30 years at 6 per cent per annum.

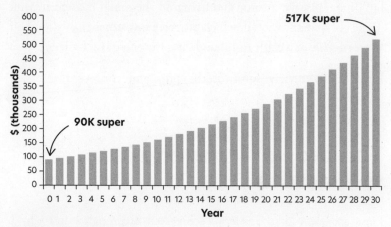

Figure 6.1: investing in a self-managed super fund without using leverage

Figure 6.2 shows how investing that $90 000 as a deposit on a $450 000 property can offer so much more.

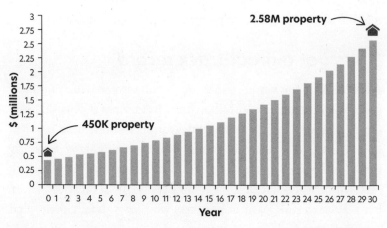

Figure 6.2: using leverage to an investor's (huge!) advantage

With property, you can win through capital growth and inflation over time, through tax deductions and benefits, and through building a passive income and living off the rental income stream. There are so many ways in which property investment can allow you to create a life of wealth and abundance. But there are challenges too.

Let's briefly review some of the pros and cons of real estate investment.

The pros of investing in real estate

Here are some of the reasons I invested in property and why I believe it's such a great way to create wealth.

1. It's physical

Unlike stocks, bonds or numbers in a bank account, property is a physical asset you can see and feel, and it most often comes with land. As Mark Twain once famously advised, 'Buy land, they aren't making it anymore.' It's a tangible asset, like gold and silver.

2. It's got a great track record

Almost all of the world's most successful entrepreneurs, business owners, millionaires and billionaires, from Robert Kiyosaki and Grant Cardone to Bill Gates and Warren Buffett, have invested in property. When I was young, while reading how famously successful people made their fortunes, I noticed they had all invested in real estate at some point in time. It's a pretty basic tip, but very powerful: learn from others who have already done what you want to do!

3. You can leverage your money

You can leverage money or use OPM (other people's money) to buy it! In some cases, you can put down as little as a 5 per cent deposit and borrow the remaining 95 per cent from a bank or financial lender. This means, for example, that when buying an investment property for $500 000 you would need to put down only $25 000 plus closing costs.

Bear in mind that lenders have different policies and rules around deposits; some will require a better LVR to offer you a mortgage. (To recap, the LVR is used by banks to describe the ratio of the loan to the value of the property: when you buy a property with a 20 per cent deposit the LVR is 80 per cent and LMI is not required.)

4. It harnesses the power of compound growth

Albert Einstein once described compound interest as 'the eighth wonder of the world'. He is reported to have observed, 'He who understands it, earns it; he who doesn't, pays it.'

I first realised the power of compound growth in my late teens when researching properties. When talking to people in their thirties and forties about property, all of them would regret that they hadn't bought in the eighties, nineties or early 2000s when it was so much cheaper. So I started researching what properties sold for 10, 15 and 20 years ago.

Compound growth is extremely powerful—we'll dive into this further using examples, graphs and charts in chapter 8.

5. It provides passive income

Investing in property is amazing because you can rent the property out for a steady return, so if it has a mortgage on it, someone else is actually paying it off for you! That's working smarter, not harder.

Over time properties that are neutral or just positively geared (meaning they have been earning enough to cover all their costs, and in some cases a little more) become even more positively geared. This is because the loan slowly reduces while the rental income slowly increases, creating passive income for you. When you own multiple properties, this can become enough to replace your wage. This is huge! Most people still adopt an old-school mentality. Their aim is to buy their own home, pay it off, work until they're 70+ years old and hope they have enough superannuation to support them in retirement.

It's about working smarter, not harder. If billionaires use this strategy to create more wealth and financial freedom, why can't you or I?

6. There are tax deductions

Investing in property can generate amazing tax deductions, which can help you make more money in the short and long term. For example, any cosmetic or structural repairs to your investment property can be tax deductible off your income. Your primary dwelling, on the other hand, enjoys no tax advantages for repairs, maintenance or renovations.

7. You have multiple options

Another reason I love property is the options it offers investors. There are many ways of investing in real estate, which we will review in the following chapter. Most of the different strategies can be classified as either *active investing* or *passive investing*.

Active investing means actively adding value to your investment, such as by developing it. You might, for example, buy an old house on a large block, knock it down and build a duplex either to on-sell for profit or to keep for rental returns. If your strategy is to search for and develop new properties to create lump-sum profits, property investment becomes your vocation.

Passive investing, on the other hand, sees an investor establishing their property portfolio for cash flow and growth, so they can eventually live off the passive income through their property portfolio income. They are not actively continuing to purchase, develop, sell, flip or renovate to create income. For example, if an investor's property portfolio brings in an annual income of $400000, and the annual expenses — including loan repayments, council rates, water rates, insurance, strata and maintenance, and tax — come to $250000, they have a net income of $150000 per year.

8. It provides housing for people

Being a property investor means making a positive contribution to society, which is why governments offer tax deductions to encourage property investment.

Over the past 13 years, while I've been so passionate about property investment, I've heard my fair share of haters, with people saying property investment is a bad thing. Landlords inflate property prices, making it harder for people to break into the property market and buy their first home. I believe this is wrong. Property investors provide homes for people who may not be in the position to buy their own home. A thousand different factors come into play, but the bottom line is that the government can't provide housing for everyone (like the public housing I grew up in). It needs independent investors to build, develop and buy residential properties to keep up with the ever-growing demand for housing.

9. It creates a legacy for your family

I wanted to help my future children so they wouldn't have to experience what I went through growing up in an extremely poor family.

It's not a pleasant conversation or thing to think about, but the reallocation of your assets and effects should be planned for through the drawing up of a will. When your solicitor or financial adviser speaks with your family after your death, by far the most significant item to be disposed of will be property. Cars, furniture, clothes, electronics and other personal items rarely appreciate in value, so they cannot be classified as an asset and do not produce income or generate tax deductions.

10. Investing in property can set you free!

Property investing is a means to an end. When I was young I saw investing in property as a way to set me free from having to work until I was 70 years old. My first seven years of working various jobs was fairly horrible. From age 14 to 21 I worked almost full-time hours, between 30 to 40 hours a week. (Even when I was at school, the evening shift at McDonald's was from 5 pm to 1 am.) I quickly concluded that I didn't want to have someone telling me what I could and could not do all day.

It started from the simple ambition of making enough money to retire early—very early, if I wanted to. I imagined owning multiple properties that would pay me $1000 a week from rent (that seemed a lot of money back then). In time I learned that it would be possible to create a property portfolio to replace my income and set me free from working!

Don't get me wrong. I understand that some people love their work or career. But creating an income from property investing can give you many more options in life, such as working the hours you want, spending more time with your family, taking holidays or travelling. The more income from property you have coming in, the more flexibility and options you have in life, and for me that was what I always dreamed of.

The cons of investing in property

But investing in property isn't a perfect answer. There's a downside that must be factored in too.

1. Unlike stocks, real estate isn't liquid

This means you can't easily sell it. With a stock, you can decide 'I want out' and sell it that same day. With property, it's a process that takes weeks to months.

2. There are ongoing costs

With stocks, you buy them and that's it — there are no other costs. With property, you need to pay for maintenance, rates, water supply, agent's fee, insurance and so on. Of course, if you select a property that is cash flow positive (as I recommend), the rent will cover all these expenses.

3. It requires management

Unlike stocks, property needs to be managed. There are bills to pay. If the oven malfunctions, you need to arrange for it to be fixed quickly. It's not an exorbitant amount of work, but it will add up to a few hours here and there over the year.

4. Transaction costs are higher

The fees to buy stocks are quite low, especially if you buy an ETF (exchange traded fund) like the ASX 200. In contrast, when you buy a property you have to pay stamp duty, and when you sell you have to pay capital gains tax.

5. There are no guarantees

Of course, this is true of stocks, property and every investment option there is. You can do your research, but there's never a guarantee. Unforeseen events happen. We can't predict the future, which is why investing is (for some) always exciting! There's no such thing as a sure thing, but with a well-thought-out strategy and thorough execution, you can minimise your risks significantly.

6. You need a chunk of savings to get started

You can start investing in shares with $100 or $5000. With property, you first need to save a deposit—usually 5 to 10 per cent.

CHAPTER 7

Other real estate strategies

There are many different real estate investment strategies. In this chapter we'll run through the main ones.

Flipping houses

Flipping houses is a popular strategy among handy and creative investors. They buy a property, maybe knock out a wall, put in a new kitchen, rip up the floor coverings to sand the hardwood underneath and repaint the whole place. Then they get it staged, put it back on the market and, *voilà*, it looks so much better and sells for considerably more than they bought it for.

But this strategy, in my opinion, isn't a great way to achieve financial freedom, for the following reasons:

- **It costs a lot.** You have to buy the property, pay stamp duty, then pay for the renovations (materials and labour). Even if you do them yourself, they will eat into your time when you could be earning money.

- **It takes a lot of time.** Even if you pay tradespeople to do all the actual work, you have to choose what renovations to take on and make any number of decisions around materials, cabinetry, fittings and finishes. On top of that, you need to find tradespeople and manage all the work being done to check it's up to scratch.

- **It can cause stress.** Flipping is often a stressful process, with a great deal of uncertainty around how much you will be able to sell a renovated property for, and it's almost inevitable that things will go wrong during the renovations, keeping you up at night.

- **You might not make any money.** After you've paid for all expenses, and you finally sell the property, how much money have you made? Was it actually worth it? Sadly, sometimes you'll find that it wasn't. You might even lose money.

Still, there are also advantages to this strategy:

- People experienced in renovations can do a great job and make a quick, decent profit.

- With the completion of each project you gain more knowledge and more connections in the building trade, which will help you do a better job on the next property, and perhaps make a bigger profit.

The main reason I don't adopt this strategy is that it means missing out on long-term growth. It's great to make a small profit now, but imagine how much that property could be worth in 10, 20 or 30 years! The odds are you'll be kicking yourself for selling it.

I've heard this sentiment expressed by many property renovators and flippers—even those who made hundreds of thousands or even millions over the years. In essence, a property is an inflationary asset that provides a rental income and tax deductions. If you put the money you make from the sale of a property in the bank, the return the bank will give you will be wretched, and it can't be leveraged.

All things considered, I believe that most of the time the strategy to buy, renovate and flip isn't worth it. Far better to buy a property under market value by 15 to 25 per cent and create instant equity without physically doing anything. At the same time, you'll make even more money from 'time in the market'. The only reason people sell quickly is to 'cash out' on the money they've made. Better instead to keep the property and still cash out by using the equity for a deposit on another investment! *And* get to hold the property over the long term and reap the reward of increased value over time.

Build new

Another strategy is to build a brand-new property then sell it for a profit, or hold it and use the equity to buy more. In my experience beginner investors who try this strategy fail nine times out of ten, wasting both time and money.

Here are some of the reasons why:

- When you build new, you pay for all the quality inclusions — the dishwasher, luxury ensuite, special lighting and flooring. Often, like a new car driven straight off the lot, the value of these inclusions can be lost within weeks of someone living in it.

- The build almost always takes longer than everyone expects. There are weather delays or supplier delays or mistakes are made — somehow, something always manages to upturn the schedule of what is already a drawn-out process. And while this is happening your money is tied up, which means your borrowing capacity with banks and lenders is also tied up! For example, if you have a $500000 new build loan for a property that is in the process of being built, there's no rental income coming in yet, so if you wanted to buy another property because an amazing deal just came up, you couldn't. (The banks won't consider rental income that has yet to materialise, so your borrowing capacity is greatly reduced when you build new.)

- It's hard to find a great location because there's simply no land available in the places where people want to live, which is why most new builds are done on the outskirts of cities. (And if you buy a rundown house closer to the city to knock down and build new, you have to pay for the demolition of the existing house too.)

- Most new builds start off negatively geared because they don't produce enough rental return to cover the mortgage and all other costs. This means you *lose* money every month as you wait for it eventually to become positively geared.

- New builds are usually done on smaller parcels of land, with smaller bedrooms and backyards, which means in 20 years' time it won't sell for as much as an existing house on a bigger block, with bigger rooms and a backyard the kids can play in.

- It's stressful. In most cases, building new is a headache, full of uncertainty, unforeseen costs and sleepless nights. Why bother when you can buy an existing property, usually for less money on a bigger block, that will be cash flow positive and give you a great sale price in decades to come?

There are also potential positives, though:

- When you build you will likely have access to government incentives, including the first home owner grant, if you are a first-time buyer.

- If you build then hold onto the property as an investment (rather than selling), you can utilise the full depreciation deductions, which can save you a lot of tax.

Buy, subdivide and sell for a profit

You may have the opportunity to convert one block into two or more. For example, someone who owns a house on an acre of land may decide to divide half of their land into four blocks of 500 square metres each. They can then sell each of these on an individual title to others to build a house on. For investors, subdivision usually occurs when a smaller block (say, 1000 square metres) has the backyard subdivided and then sold as land. The other option is for an old existing house on a suburban block to be knocked down and cleared, and the land then divided in two. Often, two adjoining townhouses are built and then sold.

If you are interested in the first option—wow, you're lucky to have found such a big block! If this is the home you have lived in for 20 years, it can be a good way to make some easy money. But if you want to buy a one-acre property to subdivide it, it often isn't worth it. Why? Because the cost of the land itself will be through the roof! These days everyone is clued up on subdivision, so the person selling the large block can charge a hefty price, and often they'll make a bigger margin than the person doing all the hard work with council around getting it subdivided.

Personally, I don't recommend going down the subdivision path if you don't already have a few properties under your belt. Even now, with my large property portfolio, I still haven't utilised this strategy.

Subdivision involves a lot more variables that can affect your return, and many things that are out of your control can go wrong. The process can be extremely drawn out, and ultimately it will be up to council whether or not it's approved.

If you do want to subdivide, here are some questions to consider:

- Is it a house on a large parcel of land, where the property can be rented out in the meantime while you deal with the headaches of trying to get approval for subdivision?

- What are the holding costs for this property while you are organising everything?

- What are your gross and net profit going to look like after you've done everything, and is there room for error?

- Based on the gross and net profit margins, what are the associated risks involved with doing this?

- If you are considering knocking down an old house to put up multiple townhouses, double-check all of the numbers. How many years will you have a property that is making you no money and instead is costing you lots? Is all of that lost time really worth it?

If you've considered all this and still think you want to go ahead, you need to be aware of the following:

- Subdivided blocks are smaller in size, which means they are usually less attractive to buyers.

- Subdivision reduces the value of the original house (if you've left it standing), which once had a nice big backyard and now has only a small front yard with another house right behind it.

- There can be unexpected costs. As with flipping houses and building new, you always need to be prepared for unexpected costs—for example, tree removal or connecting services such as water, power and sewerage.

- It's very slow. Subdividing usually takes longer than renovations—and we all know how they can drag on! When you do your research with council to determine how long the process will take, always add at least six months as a buffer.

- There may be objections from neighbours. A neighbour who loves the view to the city over your backyard is likely to object strongly to a house being built there. Neighbours can delay, and sometimes even halt, subdivisions, so it's a risk that needs to be considered.

Granny flats

Do I have properties with granny flats on them in my personal property portfolio? Yes, I do! However, I didn't buy the property and then build the granny flat, I bought properties that already included an established granny flat.

Because building a granny flat in a backyard is cheaper than buying a block and building a new house, it can seem appealing, but I personally don't recommend it. Why? Because nearly all investors do this based on emotion and not actual numbers. Many fall in love with the idea of getting their hands dirty and building something from the ground up. Unfortunately for most, once complete, the numbers don't add up. In my experience, building a brand-new granny flat on an existing property has more cons than pros.

As usual it will depend on their situation and experience, but for most investors who don't already own six to ten properties, I believe it's a mistake to go down this path. While the rental return might seem huge, the downside is the cost of the build and the capital return. Usually you can't leverage a granny flat's costs, so if it costs roughly $120000 to build (including approvals, sewerage and so on), you will either have to dip into your savings or use equity capital to pay for it. Instead, you could have used that $120000 to buy a couple more investment properties!

If I was an investor with just three properties in my portfolio, I would prefer to use $120000 capital to buy three separate properties with 10 per cent deposits — $40000 per deposit. Using these numbers, I could buy three $300000 properties that were 20 per cent under market value, so each property would be worth roughly $360000. Doing so would add a total of $1080000 worth of property to my portfolio, doubling the number of properties I have! This marks the difference between a *scale mindset* and a *consolidate mindset*.

Here are some other considerations:

- Much like building new or flipping houses, building a granny flat can precipitate lots of time, work, money, stress and budget blow-outs.

- Some states and territories in Australia won't let you build a granny flat unless you can prove a family member needs to live there, and many councils outright don't allow granny flat plans.

- If you build a granny flat with the plan of renting it out, expect that it can take longer to find a tenant. Most people prefer to rent a house with their own little backyard than to live in a flat in someone else's backyard.

- Granny flats usually don't add any equity value to the property above the build cost.

- If you are renting out the front house while the granny flat is constructed, you may have to accept less rent from your existing tenant because of the disruptions during construction and then the annoyance of having someone else live in what had been their rented backyard.

Still, there are some positives:

- They provide extra cash flow.

- You get two sources of income from the rental property, diversifying your risk.

- You can depreciate the granny flat build, as you do when you build a new house, which can save you tax.

Another potential positive is that granny flats add to your serviceability for future loans. However, I would only try to increase cash flow by adding a secondary dwelling / granny flat if I had already leveraged my capital to the fullest and needed more. For example, an investor owns nine properties, and several of them have granny flat potential. The investor is struggling with the banks for their serviceability. In that situation, constructing two or three granny flats would be useful for servicing, and they have already built a good-sized portfolio of nine properties worth, say, $4 million.

Buying a house with an already established granny flat is much better than buying a property and building one yourself. I bought an established house and granny flat for $309 000, with a combined rent of $500+ per week. An investor could buy that with as little as 5 or 10 per cent deposit plus purchasing costs, so with a 5 per cent deposit and another 5 per cent for purchasing costs, they would have got this property for only $30 900. If, however, they bought a comparable property for $250 000 and did the same, with 10 per cent all up to purchase, this would demand $25 000 buying costs. Then they build a granny flat, spending all the time and effort and funds of roughly $120 000. They can't leverage the building costs, which means they would have to put in total capital of $145 000 cash!

For me, if you're a serious investor striving towards financial freedom, nine times out of ten, buying a property then building a granny flat makes no sense.

Wrapping properties

Wrapping is common in the US and other countries, but is not widely practised in Australia. It involves getting finance to buy a property under market value, then on-selling it at market price to a buyer who is unable to secure a traditional loan. You charge the buyer slightly more interest (1.5 to 2 per cent) than you are paying on your loan. Hence the buyer's interest charge essentially 'wraps' the interest you are paying.

I think this is a lousy strategy. I would never waste time trying to do a wrap for a measly 2 to 4 per cent net profit. I have read lots of books on it and have met many investors who have tried to adopt the strategy because it seemed interesting and original. All of these investors got stuck with serviceability with the banks, and in time usually regretted on-selling the property and therefore losing the asset!

They are essentially locking up their own borrowing capacity and serviceability and giving up future capital growth for a small short-term gain. In 10 to 15 years' time they'll look back and regret their decision. If bought in the right metro market, the property would have doubled in value and they would have missed out on all the capital growth and future opportunities.

Commercial real estate

For the investor, commercial real estate is quite different from residential real estate. I usually advise people to stick with residential, as there are added complexities and costs associated with commercial property.

Here are some of the reasons why I don't recommend it:

- **More tax.** When you buy a commercial property, you often have to pay the purchase price plus GST.

- **Long leases.** Commercial lease agreements are usually much longer than residential leases. Five years, or even ten, is common.

- **Long vacancies.** The time between tenants is often much longer for commercial properties.

- **High price tag.** Commercial properties are usually more expensive to invest in. For example, in the Brisbane suburb of Springwood you can buy a townhouse for $200000 (and rent it for $330 a week), but a commercial property in that same suburb (depending on size) might cost $400000 or more, plus the extra deposit costs.

- **Extra deposit costs.** Commercial property deposits are generally 30 per cent or more, so the upfront savings required are significantly higher, which impedes your ability to buy, as well as slowing down the purchase of a second and third property.

The one positive is that some expenses are covered by the tenant. For example, with a residential property the owner pays for rates and water supply, whereas with a commercial lease the tenant pays for these things. This means more money in your back pocket, but I've found the average yields for commercial properties are on a par with those for residential properties (averaging 7 to 9 per cent).

I strongly recommend you first master residential property investing before venturing into commercial property. In my experience, residential properties are safer and more predictable because of supply and demand. There are more people looking for rental properties to live in than businesses needing space. I've seen commercial properties sit vacant for years at a time, whereas residential properties usually attract a new tenant within weeks (sometimes days).

Part of scaling a property investment portfolio comes from the ability to recycle capital and extract it from current properties you have, which you bought below market value. With residential properties the major banks often have four different ways of doing a valuation (covered in chapter 10), which you can use to your advantage. With commercial properties, however, the banks usually apply just one type of valuation: the full valuation.

CHAPTER 8

My property strategy

The overall strategy that has guided me from my very first purchases, and has proved itself time and time again over the years, can be summed up by the following three principles.

Buy for capital growth, cash flow positive and under market value

My golden rule is to buy residential properties in a growth area that are under market value and have high yields. I began by focusing on buying investment properties that fit this description. I didn't limit my search to stand-alone houses or houses with at least *x* square metres of land. Such property investing 'rules' can sabotage your ability to build a property portfolio that is cash flow positive from day one.

1. Buy properties below market value

This is essential. Buying a property below what it is currently worth leaves nothing to chance. You're not 'hoping' it will go up—you *know* from day one it is worth more. You have instant equity, which creates a great buffer in case the market starts to fall, and you have an exit strategy if needed—you can sell it to free up some cash and can still turn a profit after paying the associated costs of doing so.

When done correctly this strategy will allow you to revalue the property relatively quickly, depending on what percentage deposit you use, allowing you to release the equity to use on your next purchase. Follow this golden rule, and you're well on your way to building a cash-flow-positive portfolio.

All my properties fit with this strategy: I bought most of them between 10 and 20 per cent below market value. (Sometimes it's even possible to buy 30 to 40 per cent below market value.) To simplify, let's assume that in your $3 million property portfolio each property was bought at an average of 15 per cent below market value comparable to similar sales. That would mean your portfolio is really worth $3 450 000! Just in the *buying* stage you've made more money than many people do in dabbling in property for years!

The two key things that set people free financially are equity growth and cash flow.

So let's assume we bought ten properties at a 90 per cent LVR.

Total value = $3.45 million.

Loans of 90 per cent of $3 million = $2.7 million in loans, which is tax deductible debt.

$3.45 million – $2.7 million

= $750 000 total equity.

By buying below market value and having strength in numbers (ten properties), we have turned $300 000 into $750 000. And this is assuming zero capital growth occurred during the building of this portfolio.

2. Buy properties with good cash flow

Good cash flow means the property not only is positively geared, but is making a bit extra for you each year as well. An overall gross yield of 5 to 10 per cent is considered very good, though obviously the higher, the better.

Most property investment experts discuss the differences between growth and cash flow properties. They explain that growth properties are located close to the CBD in major cities, and cash flow properties are based in regional areas. In my view, this paints an incorrect picture.

There are, and always will be, emerging property markets within 45 minutes of a CBD with cash-flow-positive residential properties. You just need to know how and where to look.

High-yielding properties provide positive cash flow from day one. If you buy a $400 000 property with a rental income of $600 per week, that 7.8 per cent yield will provide you with thousands every year in positive cash flow. This means this hard-earned income isn't going towards supporting your investment property and can instead be put towards saving a deposit to buy your next property—as can the passive income your property is making for you! It also gives you a safety buffer in case interest rates rise.

Right now in 2021 interest rates are between 2 and 3 per cent, but in the past they were much higher. If interest rates were to rise to 7 per cent, a lot of investors who had bought properties at the lower rates would be in financial trouble. They would either have to start paying out of their personal income to support the property or sell it urgently to rid themselves of the negatively geared investment. (If interest rates rose quickly, some could even face bankruptcy, with the property repossessed.)

So which properties are usually positively geared? Units and townhouses tend to have higher yields because they are cheaper to buy but can still deliver a good rent, though they do generally have strata and body corporate fees to cover. By comparison, houses almost always have lower gross yields, but they can often (not always) enjoy better growth. In my property portfolio I have a combination of houses, duplexes, townhouses and units.

Many investors get stuck with finance when they buy low-yielding or negatively geared properties. They may have three or four properties and want to buy another, but the banks analyse their cash flow position, along with their personal income, and see them as too risky to lend to. The lower the yield, the lower the future borrowing capacity.

After buying properties in Sydney for between $700 000 and $1.3 million that were initially negatively geared or had low gross yields to start with, I had to make sure my subsequent purchases had extremely high rental yields to compensate. Ensuring that you have good overall cash flow in your portfolio is crucial. So if you buy a few properties in Sydney or Melbourne that are likely negatively geared to begin with, you must then diversify by buying a few properties with 7 to 9 per cent yields or better, perhaps in Brisbane or Adelaide, so your property portfolio works together as a whole.

To summarise, ensuring your property portfolio is sound from a cash flow perspective has the following benefits:

- It provides you with passive income.

- It provides you with a safety buffer should interest rates rise or unexpected issues crop up.

- It provides you with the ability to continue building your property portfolio from a finance perspective; the more cash flow you have compared with your recurring expenses, the more investment properties you will continue to get loans for, and the further your investing journey can go.

3. Capital growth

Buying properties that will experience capital growth is a crucial part of the investing formula. Many people believe that if you buy a property with a higher yield, you have to sacrifice capital growth. As I've said, this isn't true at all. Out of the 30+ properties I own, almost all of them are close (within 40 kilometres) to a major capital city such as Sydney, Brisbane, the Gold Coast or Adelaide, and *all* have experienced significant capital growth.

Overall long-term capital growth gives you that equity uplift that (1) increases the overall value of your portfolio, (2) makes servicing new loans easier because your LVR on existing properties improves, and (3) means you can release equity to use in buying more properties, growing your property portfolio.

From a tax perspective, capital growth is fantastic because you don't pay tax on the gain until you sell the property. So if you hold on to a property forever, and turn the equity into cash as needed, you get the hard cash benefit of the increased value of the property without paying capital gains tax. The ability to defer capital gains tax on the gains made each year is extraordinary.

A good way to ensure you can ride the capital growth wave is to buy in different states. Each state is at different phases of the property clock (as explained in chapter 12), and can do different things at different times according to the supply and demand within that market, as well as many other factors.

Compound growth

Compound growth is one of the biggest advantages of property investing, as it can help you create enormous wealth. It's important to understand how it works and the benefits it will deliver over the long term. In essence, *compound growth* describes consistent gains, year on year, from an investment. Figure 8.1 shows how a $3 million property portfolio will grow over 30 years at 6 per cent per annum.

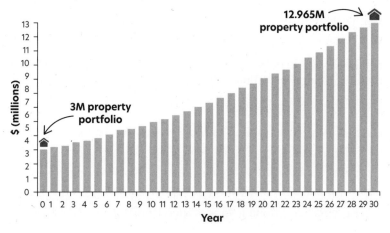

Figure 8.1: the power of compound interest

My parents' former property in Mount Druitt is a good example of compound growth. Having been purchased for $50 000 in the late 1980s, it would have doubled to $100 000 in the first decade, which would then double again to $200 000 in the next, then to $400 000, and so on. If only they had held on to it!

There are obviously variables to take into account. Growth rarely follows a straight line.

A common expression in investing circles is, 'It's not about timing the market, it's about time in the market'. Figure 8.2 shows how median Australian house and unit prices have fared over the past 25 years.

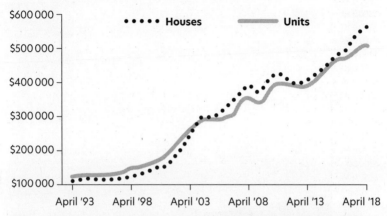

Figure 8.2: property price increases between 1993 and 2018
Source: based on data from CoreLogic, RBA, ABS.

This graph demonstrates that since 1993, Australian house prices have increased by 412 per cent, and units by 316 per cent.

Hypothetically, if my parents had bought five similar properties in the 1980s and rented the remaining four out, they would have had $250 000 worth of assets with $200 000 to $225 000 worth of debt against the entire portfolio. If they had ensured the properties were cash flow positive, the rent would have generally exceeded their expense commitments over the years, increasing naturally over time due to inflation and eventually paying off the loan. Today they would have assets worth over $2.5 million and no debt.

Sounds so simple, right? It truly does come down to the fundamentals of housing markets and inflation over time. Figure 8.3 (overleaf) represents visually how compound growth is achieved over time.

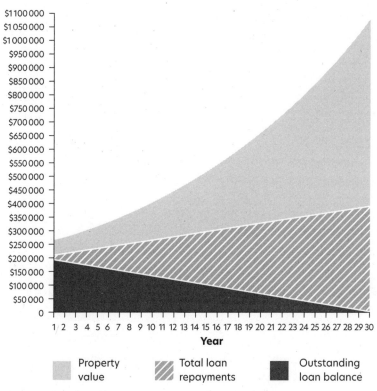

Figure 8.3: the power of compound growth and leverage over time

Over a 30-year period you may see:

- the loan amount reducing, along with your debt

- principal repayments rising as the interest falls

- property value (and therefore your wealth) increasing.

We cannot know where Australian house prices will be in 25+ years, as there are too many variables that will affect them. However, if capital gains were to continue at the same rate as in the previous 25 years, modelling from CoreLogic suggests that the median Australian house price could hit $2.9 million, from a median of roughly $809 000 today. Interesting to think about, right? To learn more about the past trends and future predictions of the Australian property market, I recommend reading the Aussie/CoreLogic report *25 Years of Housing Trends*, available online, which explores this in more detail.

My first property on the Central Coast jumped from $138 500 to $300 000 within five years, which is a great (though not necessarily predictable) outcome. It also experienced a 50 per cent increase in rental return, rising from $200 to $300 a week.

This is why I constantly stress the importance of buying affordable metro properties in the outer rings and some inner rings of major cities, buying below market value and ensuring positive cash flow to reduce risk and build your wealth. If you can manage to accumulate five properties like this at $400 000 each, you will have $2 million in gross assets. Hang on to them long term, let the compound growth and inflation do its thing, and you will be thanking yourself later. As illustrated in the following two graphs (figures 8.4 and 8.5, both overleaf), it really does come down to time. This example shows a $2 million property portfolio growing at a rate of 5 per cent per annum.

We'll end this chapter with a look at another acquisition that illustrates the principles I've outlined here.

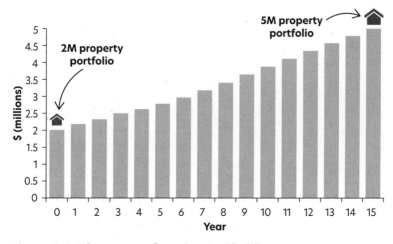

Figure 8.4: The power of owning and holding a property portfolio

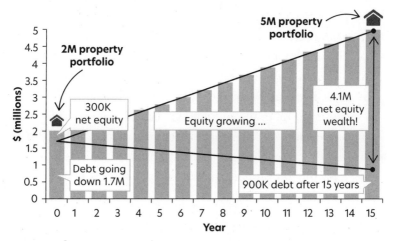

Figure 8.5: how investors create wealth over time

A perfect fit: another great property example

This property, which I bought in April 2020 for $565 000, met my three key criteria perfectly, being below market value with great growth potential and a good rental yield. I found it through a real estate agent I had bought another property from a year before. He told me about a dual occupancy property on a corner block of roughly 700 sqm that needed to be sold as soon as possible. We were all in COVID lockdown at the time, so I was able to buy it at significantly under market value. As a dual-occupancy property with two incomes, it had a very strong cash flow position plus tax depreciation benefits.

Table 8.1 shows how the numbers stacked up.

Table 8.1: calculations for a duplex property bought in 2020

Estimated expenses	Weekly ($)	Monthly ($)	Annually ($)
Council rates	34.62	150.00	1800.00
Strata fees inc. building insurance	–	–	–
Water rates	26.92	116.67	1400.00
Building insurance	15.38	66.67	800.00
Management fees	36.54	158.33	1900.00
Mortgage repayments (current interest rate)	230.77	1000.00	12000.00
Landlord insurance	9.62	41.67	500.00
Estimated totals	**353.85**	**1533.33**	**18400.00**
Income comparables			
Lower rent	770.00	3336.67	40040.00
Higher rent	800.00	3466.67	41600.00
Estimated cash flow before tax			
Lower rent	416.50	1803.33	21640.00
Higher rent	446.15	1933.33	23200.00

A huge duplex on a corner block

There are still so many great properties out there. You haven't missed the boat!

PART III

YOUR INVESTMENT JOURNEY

Now for the exciting part—your journey! I am passionate about the work I do helping all kinds of people buy investment properties. It's so rewarding watching them build their wealth when they previously thought they couldn't. So let's dive into your own property investment journey.

CHAPTER 9
Your goals

I want to reiterate that this book is not a golden ticket to wealth. There's no magic formula for getting rich quick. Sorry, it just doesn't work like that! You're going to have to work hard.

Throughout the book I talk about using equity to buy more properties. That might make it sound easy, but it's important to remember that along the way I worked two or three jobs at a time. I put in long hours, sometimes up to 90 per week. I constantly sought ways to increase my income and bring in extra money I could put towards a deposit. I lived very frugally, forgoing unnecessary expenses such as new clothes, shoes and depreciating assets. I made lots of sacrifices along the way.

Building a property portfolio takes time and hard work. It can be complicated, confusing and sometimes risky. However, it is worth it. And with the right tools, the right motivation and a solid plan, it doesn't have to be all work and no play. Having fun and enjoying yourself is important when building your portfolio, and indeed is imperative for your success.

It is 100 per cent possible to create a life you love and a future you deserve — you just have to be smart about it. I've said it before: if I can do it, anyone can.

Understanding property investing

It took years for me to understand all the ways property can set a person free. In the beginning I saw property investing as a side hustle, a way to work towards building a better future for myself and for my family. Over the years I discovered that property investing can itself be a way of life.

As in a game of Monopoly, there can be wins and losses, but by the end, the winner is the one who holds the most real estate. Unlike Monopoly, though, landing on a piece of real estate doesn't depend on a roll of the dice. You do your research before making your decisions.

Sometimes too much information can work against you. When I first started, I didn't know 5 per cent of what I know now, but that didn't keep me from getting started. Looking back, it was just as well there were far fewer property investment books and informational videos to keep up with than there are today.

Don't get me wrong. I researched for weeks, months, even years before I bought my first property, but I still could have done much more, and I'm glad I didn't. Too many people today overanalyse and then get stuck with analysis paralysis, and end up doing nothing at all!

If I were starting all over again I'd use the same approach, which is to start small and grow over time. This eliminates much of the risk.

For example, your first investment property might be a $700 000 house that rents out for $500 a week (for a horrible yield of 3.71 per cent). Alternatively, you could start off with a smaller house, townhouse or unit in the same location for only $350 000 that rents for $400 a week (for a better yield of 5.9 per cent). This is where most people go wrong. They assume the more expensive property is the better option because it will enjoy more capital growth. In my experience, this is nonsense!

When considering growth, most people don't focus on the percentages, so they are blind to what's really going on. They make their judgement based on the value and emotion tied up in the property itself. For example, imagine that over the next 15 years the same two properties double in value. The $700 000 property is now valued at $1.4 million and the $350 000 property is worth $700 000. Most people would say the first property grew more, but in reality the properties grew by the same percentage and made the same percentage profit.

Some people might say, well, I'd rather own the $1.4 million property, but they don't look at the holding costs and negative cash flow. During its years of growth you're losing money—often hundreds of dollars every month! This not only diminishes your profit when you sell, but it also hinders your ability to buy other investment properties in the interim. I would rather buy two properties for $350 000 each than one for $700 000. The yield for the $350 000 property is much better, in this case 5.9 per cent (compared with 3.71 per cent). Furthermore, with two properties you can diversify your investment by buying in two different locations and spread the risk across two different tenants, so it's far safer.

As my portfolio has grown over time, I have made larger purchases, sometimes with lower yields, to balance my portfolio in terms of locations. But to begin, particularly for your first six properties, it's important to focus on all three keys: under market value, capital growth and higher yields. Always begin small (with more affordable properties that have higher yields, are under market value and enjoy capital growth) and gradually build up over time as you become more experienced.

With a sound foundation to your property portfolio, you can start to explore different options and perhaps even branch out into development or bulk unit purchases. A very experienced property investor can begin buying larger assets that have a different level of risk and reward, such as buying unit blocks of 10, 20 or 40 units at a time. Crucially, they always have the solid foundation of their initial properties to rely on.

What is your end goal?

Start with a clear understanding of your objective. What is your ultimate goal? Is it to:

- become financially free
- live life on your own terms
- be able to do what you want when you want
- be able to spend more time with your family and friends
- have enough money to travel and enjoy new experience
- take care of your family financially?

I've found that the best way to reach your goal is to put a number on it. Not only will it help you shape your strategy, but it will hold you accountable if you come up short. Many people I speak with don't like putting a number on how many properties they want to have in their portfolio or how much equity or cash flow they want to generate each year. They themselves don't really know what they are reaching for! I believe this is why most of them fail to achieve their financial goals through property investment. It's like driving at night and trying to figure out where you're going with no road map.

What annual passive income will allow you to reach your goal? Whatever your goal, you need to put a monetary figure on it. Money doesn't solve all our problems, but it certainly helps!

Think about some possible financial goals for the next 10 years of investing in property. Is it to earn a passive income of $50000 a year? Or $100000? Or $1 million? Is it to sell all your properties and, after paying taxes, bank $2 to $3 million? Would that amount be enough to live off comfortably for the rest of your life?

Once you know your goal, you can work out your strategy to achieve it. Let's say, as an example, you want to generate a passive income of $100000. How many properties will you need in your property portfolio? Is it two, five, eight or even 20 or more? To figure this out you need to 'reverse engineer' your goal.

There are, of course, many ways you could achieve this passive income, but let's focus on the basic one first: the old-school approach of buying properties and paying them off, so all the rent becomes income. For example, if you had five investment properties renting out for $500 per week each and they were all completely paid off, you would be making $2500 a week in gross income.

Now, to get down to the nitty-gritty, not all of that would be passive income as properties always have holding expenses. We will dive into this issue more thoroughly later, but the basics you'll need to cover include council rates, water rates, management fees, insurance and maintenance. These could demand as much as $500 per week, meaning your $2500 per week income would shrink to $2000 per week. Multiplying that by 52 weeks gives you an annual passive income of $104 000.

By now you're probably thinking, that sounds simple enough, but how the hell do I get five investment properties to begin with? And how do I pay them off? Won't that take 30 years for each property? I don't want to wait that long! If that's close to what you're thinking, then good, because you're on the right track. Later we'll go deep into how you can create a passive income from building a sustainable property portfolio, with detailed strategies on ways you can speed things up and get the passive income coming in a lot sooner than the basic example above.

What is your why?

Being armed with the right knowledge and information is one thing, but to really achieve your goals you also need to be motivated and ready to work for it. Identifying your *why* is the single most important and powerful force that will drive you to push harder, think smarter, do the research and make the sacrifices necessary to create your future.

I've already shared with you some of the challenges of growing up poor. Not knowing whether we could make it to the next pay day, dreading the surprise expense that could cripple our family budget for months, sometimes not even knowing where our next meal was coming from—it was a stressful way to live. It could have been so easy to remain trapped in that cycle, but I wanted more, and I wanted better for my future family. The determination to change my circumstances is what first made me want to learn about property investment and to begin my wealth-creation journey. It was my reason *why*.

Whether you want more freedom to travel and party, to pursue your creative interests, to work less, to retire early or simply to provide a comfortable lifestyle for you and your family, keeping your *why* at the front of your mind as you read this book will help get you there.

Where are you starting from?

Let's be honest, optimistic and realistic all at the same time. Property investment, as I've made clear, is not a get-rich-quick scheme. It's not something that can happen overnight. It takes time, dedication and hard work. That said, just like anything else in life, once you get the hang of it, it can become fun and easy.

I am where I am today for a number of reasons, one of which is that I started at a very young age. Even if you aren't starting your journey as an 18-year-old, though, you can still look forward to a life of wealth and abundance through property investing.

Property investment as a wealth-creation strategy can be looked at as a journey, and the first step is to identify clearly where you are right now and where you want to be ultimately. The next important question is: what is the length of time you are going to aim for to complete this journey?

Also consider what sacrifices you are willing to make to shorten your journey. In my opinion, seven to ten years makes a good target, but of course it can be longer or shorter depending on your position and goals.

How many properties do you need to build a passive income stream to live off?

As with most answers in property investment, it starts with, 'well, it depends ...', in this case on your circumstances and goals. As a general guide, I recommend people who want to replace their income should aim for a portfolio of a minimum of six properties. (Fewer than 1 per cent of property investors ever get to the point of owning more than six properties.)

If you own six investment properties worth around $400000 each, that's a $2.4 million portfolio. If each property has a net annual yield of 6 per cent (for example, if the weekly rent is $600), then each property is likely to be positively geared by about $10000 a year, depending on interest rates. That means that in the early years, those six properties could provide you with $50000 to $60000 of passive income a year after all expenses, and over time this could increase significantly as rents rise with inflation and your loans are gradually reduced.

After 15 years you could hypothetically sell two properties, which, conservatively, would have now doubled in value. After the selling costs and capital gains tax, this could potentially pay out the remaining loans, which means you own the remaining four properties (worth roughly $3 million) outright! Of course, the exact number of properties you should aim for depends on many factors, such as your income and the quality of the properties you purchase.

But how do I get started?

Write down your current income per week, month and year, and calculate your expenses. Whether you're searching for your first investment property or buying your third or sixth, ensuring you fully understand your current income and expenditure position is extremely important! It involves examining your personal financial position forensically. Set up a budget to see where your money is moving from and to.

I created my first budget when working at KFC and McDonald's by hand-writing it on scrap paper. It showed how much I was making each week, how much tax I had to pay, what expenses I had and how much I had left over to save for investments. I eventually upgraded to an Excel spreadsheet. (For a copy of my Property Investment Budget Template, head to dilleenproperty. com.au or email admin@dilleenpg.com to request a copy.)

Now let's do the math to calculate how long it will take you to buy your first property. Having written down your income and expenses, calculate how much you can save each week towards a property investment deposit. For example, if you can save $500 a week from your income, you will have saved $26 000 after just one year.

Now, depending on what bank or financial lender you use, it is possible to buy a property with a 5 per cent or 10 per cent deposit. With a 5 per cent deposit, after only 12 months you could buy a property worth $250 000! Here's what the costs could look like:

Deposit (5%)	$12 500
Stamp duty	$8 000
Legal fees / bank fees/ pest and building reports	$2 000
Lenders mortgage insurance (LMI)*	$5 000
Total	**$27 500**

*Sometimes this can be added to the loan, to minimise upfront costs.

Is it best to buy a place to live in or to rentvest?

In Australia, many people who dream of owning their first home start out renting while they save for a deposit. After they have bought their home, if they're keen to invest, they'll save a deposit for an investment property. I understand why people do this, but it's a much slower way to achieve your financial goals.

Rentvesting is the strategy of renting where you want to live and investing in another property where it's best from an investment perspective. I used rentvesting as a way to build my portfolio rapidly, and if I was starting all over, I would definitely use this strategy.

For people who live in an area where property prices are high, such as closer to the CBD in Sydney or Melbourne where suburban median prices are $2 million, rentvesting makes sense. If you waited until you had enough money to buy a $2 million home, you'd be waiting years! In that time you could have already been investing, and have built up a portfolio of three to five cash-flow-positive investment properties that would be making you money!

A lot of these inner-city suburbs are simply unaffordable nowadays. If you're young and just starting out, with an income of $70000, you aren't going to be able to service a $2 million loan. Your borrowing power might be $400000 to $600000. Much better for you to rent, paying much less a month than the minimum mortgage repayments for a house in that suburb. Then you can use your savings to buy smart investments.

I didn't buy a place to live in until I had 14 investment properties under my belt.

There are pros and cons to rentvesting.

Pros:

- You can achieve your property portfolio dreams far more quickly. (If you're young, you can acquire multiple properties before you have the responsibility of children.)

- You can live where you want to.

- You can buy investment properties that fit your strategy.

- You'll have far more investment property options to choose between if you're not restricted by the need to live there one day.

- You can move around more easily and explore living in different suburbs, and even cities, to gain clarity on your ideal lifestyle and where you'd like to live.

Cons:

- The experience of living in your own home is delayed, so while friends might be throwing house-warming parties, you must stay true to your financial goals.

- Renting isn't as stable as living in your own home: you might be forced to move out at the end of your lease.

There's a common perception that rent money is 'dead money', but as long as you're smart enough to find a good rental deal and you're investing the difference in other properties, I strongly believe you're following a better strategy.

Property investing as a partnership / joint venture

If you don't have enough cash to get started on your property investment journey on your own, you might consider investing in your first property with someone else in a joint venture. This can sound like a great idea because it speeds things up, but don't jump into it without careful planning. Even if it's with a friend—in fact, *especially* if it's with a friend!—make sure you set up a watertight legal agreement. Things can go wrong, and you don't want to lose a friend or your money.

The agreement should cover what you both are going to invest in it in terms of time, money and responsibility, and very importantly, what you both want to get out of it. You need to make sure you have the same goals and timeframe. You also need to make sure you have a clear buyout clause if one of you wants to sell their share. (If you have the same goals and timeframe, hopefully this won't happen, but circumstances can change!)

The big thing to consider is, while a joint venture can help you get a foot in the door, there is a financial risk. For example, if you get a joint loan, what happens if your investment partner stops paying their share? According to the bank, you are both liable for the full repayment, so you might have to pay their part, at least for a while until you can prove the arrangement (another reason to make sure you have legal documentation before you start).

The other thing that's tricky with joint ventures is how some lenders view the loan. If you have gone halves with a friend or relative in the purchase of a rental property and have a joint mortgage of $400000, you will each view your personal debt as $200000. But the bank sees each of you as responsible for the full debt. When it comes to rental income, however, the bank will only take *your* half of the rental income into account. This has a strong negative impact on any future investments you might want to get into, because the bank sees you as someone who is already responsible for a $400 000 debt, while they view the rental income as half of what it is. (To avoid this trap, I recommend buying a property — house, unit or townhouse — that you can afford on your own, rather than buying a larger property in a joint-venture structure.)

CHAPTER 10

Understanding finance

Ensuring you have a solid understanding of the terminology and processes of finance and how it works will serve you well throughout your investment journey. Without it your chances of success are much reduced. This chapter introduces what you'll need to know.

Finance application

This is the process of obtaining finance for your property. A bank lender or broker will gather evidence of your income, marital status, dependants, monthly expenses and any rental income to satisfy themselves that you will be able to repay any loan they approve. This pre-qualifies you for a loan.

DEFINITION

Factors a prospective lender will consider include:

- your current property portfolio rental income. The yields of your properties have a big impact on your ability to make future purchases. Many investors get stuck with finance because they've bought properties with 2 to 3 per cent yields, and when the bank does their servicing, they come up short. They will view you more favourably when you buy a property with a high yield. If you already have a few properties with low yields, you can balance your portfolio by buying a couple of properties with high yields to help with future servicing.

- your living expenses, such as groceries, clothes and entertainment expenses

- any personal loans or business loans you have

- how many dependants you have, including children and a non-working partner. The bank will take into account all dependants' expenses, as well as your own, which can make borrowing harder.

- your current rent/accommodation expenses

- any HECS debt from studying at university

- your credit card limit. This will be calculated as debt, even if you currently owe nothing on the card, because it's possible for you to go and spend that money at any time.

DEFINITION

Debt servicing

Debt servicing (the payments of principal and interest you will need to make to pay off a debt) is contingent on how much a lender or broker determines you can borrow (your borrowing capacity). Most of the time this is calculated using the information provided in the application, though other factors will also come into play.

Broker or bank?

In my experience, there are advantages and disadvantages to using brokers or banks when seeking finance for your loan.

Brokers

Brokers can negotiate with a number of lenders on your behalf to get you the best deal; however, this usually comes at a price. They are also offered financial incentives by the lender for selling you certain products, so it's important to use a reputable broker who is acting not only in their best interest, but in yours too.

A big advantage of using a broker is they can order property bank evaluations up front before an application takes places—and, more importantly, before a *credit enquiry* goes on your file (more on this later).

Banks

Dealing directly with a bank gives you the opportunity to build a strong and mutually beneficial relationship with your lender. The right person can influence the credit team when your application is escalated, which can increase your chance of getting a loan approved.

In my experience, it is important to find someone who understands what you are trying to achieve and who has experience in helping investors build a portfolio. Finding someone like this is not always easy. The best approach is to meet with a handful of individuals from different banks and branches and ask lots of questions:

- How long have you been in the industry?

- What is your experience with property investing?

- Do you yourself own any investment properties?

- How many people have you helped to build a substantial property portfolio?

In addition, unlike brokers, some lenders have access to electronic valuation systems, which can help leverage the property you may be taking equity from when refinancing. The major downside to this is that most of them must prepare and lodge your application before giving you any answers. This will involve lodging a credit enquiry on your name or the entity under which you are buying the property. It is somewhat risky to seek a better valuation from a bank when shopping around, as if it turns out the same or not as high as you anticipated, you will be stuck with an unnecessary enquiry on your file, which can later impact your ability to obtain finance.

You'll need to weigh up the pros and cons of using either a broker or a bank, and make a choice that best suits your particular circumstances.

Mortgage options

If you haven't taken out a mortgage before, it can be confusing to know where to start. The banks want to sell you the product that works best for them, but that might not be the one that works best for you. Here are some of the options.

Fixed interest vs variable interest rate

When signing up for your loan, you have to choose between the current interest rate (fixed), which you will pay for an agreed length of time, and a rate that changes when interest rates are changed by the Reserve Bank (variable).

If you choose fixed, your interest rate and repayments stay the same for the agreed length of time, which may be anything from one to ten years. With a variable rate, your minimum repayment will go up if interest rates rise, and go down if interest rates fall.

With interest rates currently at a record low, you might think it's a no-brainer to go for a fixed interest rate. But there are other things to keep in mind. A fixed-rate loan might not have as many features, such as access to redraw (we'll get to that), and if you want to refinance your loan or pay out your loan early, you may be stung with a charge called a *break cost*, which can be hefty. A variable rate loan will have more flexibility in these areas, but of course there is the risk of your payments going up if interest rates rise.

If you aren't sure which is best in your circumstances, some lenders offer the option of a split rate—half fixed, half variable.

Redraw facilities vs offset accounts

If you take out a variable loan, you will probably be able to choose features such as an offset account or a redraw facility. Both of these can help you reduce the amount of interest you pay over the lifetime of the loan, and can help you pay your loan off earlier, but they work differently.

An *offset* account is a separate account into which you can deposit money, which you can then use for everyday spending. The money sitting in the account works to reduce the interest on the loan. A *redraw* is a service that lets you draw out any extra payments you have made. So if you are saving up for something, instead of putting money aside in a savings account, you make extra payments on your loan, which helps reduce the interest over time, then you draw it out when you've reached your saving goal.

From a tax perspective, offset accounts might be better for investment properties because taking money out of an offset account doesn't affect the tax deductibility of the interest you pay on the loan. A redraw facility can be a bit more complicated.

I recommend you talk to the bank about which will work best for you. You won't necessarily have to choose one or the other; some loans let you have both!

Principal and interest vs interest only

We talked a little about interest-only loans back in chapter 2. As the name suggests, for a period of time (usually no more than five years) you need only pay off the interest and associated costs. This keeps the repayments lower in the beginning, but of course there's a point when you are going to have to start paying the principal as well, which can mean a significant jump in repayments, so you really need to plan ahead to make sure you don't get stuck.

Opting for an interest-only loan can be a useful strategy if you need to free up cash, but you won't be paying the loan down from the get-go, as you will if you start with an interest and principal loan.

My advice here is to do your sums carefully, and ensure you're prepared for when the principal repayments kick in. The bank won't give you the loan if you can't afford it. They're very conservative when doing their calculations around whether you can service the loan, so you shouldn't land in hot water. But this is another reason why buying a high-yield property is important, as it ensures you can cover both the interest and principal repayments regardless of changing circumstances.

Different lenders, different policies

It's not uncommon for people to take what they are told by a broker or bank as definitive. This is a *huge* mistake. If at first you don't succeed, pick yourself up and try again.

I have been knocked back many times by different banks and lenders, who have told me that I wouldn't be able to service the debt, that I'd have to wait before buying another property, that my whole strategy was wrong and I should go about it differently. Once I understood that these individuals weren't investors with large portfolios themselves and didn't have the experience to give me the right advice, I started to second guess what I was hearing and research the facts for myself.

In my experience, different lenders have vastly different policies and lending criteria for dealing with investors. You may submit identical applications to bank A and bank B and be offered amounts that differ by hundreds of thousands of dollars, depending on their respective flexibility in relation to certain criteria. These criteria can include your work history, where favourability can be affected by factors such as how long you have worked in one place and your type of employment (casual, part time, salaried or self-employed).

Seek out a lender who will work *with you*.

Valuations

There are four major types of bank valuations that you will encounter, all of which can give you a different result for the same property. Some are more conservative, others more lenient—and you can use these to your advantage to extract capital from the properties you already own. Banking policies can always change, but in my experience the larger the bank, the more types of valuations they will generally have. For example, the big four banks will usually do all four types of valuations described next. I believe this is because, with more capital, they can tolerate a higher exposure to risk and can afford to do quicker valuations based on statistical data (rather than site visits). This may lead to a less conservative valuation.

In contrast, I have personally found that smaller second- and third-tier lenders usually rely on the full valuation method (meaning someone physically inspects the property), which can lead to a more conservative valuation. It's usually more conservative because it takes into account far more of the details of the property, such as the quality of the build, wear and tear, fixtures and fittings, street-facing angles or if the property is on a hill.

The following are the four types of valuations:

- **Full valuation.** A specialist valuer will personally inspect the property thoroughly, and compare it with market data, comparable sales and current properties for sale, before arriving at an objective decision on its worth.

- **Drive-by valuation.** A drive-by valuation is determined based on a quick, much-less-thorough drive-by inspection coupled with data such as recent comparable sales, current properties for sale and market trends.

- **Desktop valuation.** The desktop valuation determines a property's value based on the available data, estimates of similar properties in the area and comparable sales.

- **Automated valuation report (AVR) or automated valuation model (AVM).** This valuation tool provides an 'instant' property value based purely on statistics, and can be even more lenient than a desktop valuation. It combines unique, real-time proprietary data (using sales figures and statistics from RP Data) with advanced predictive modelling. If the estimated value the owner gives falls within their 'range of value' based on their stats, they will simply accept it as the value.

The different characteristics of these valuation methods mean they can sometimes return a different valuation, depending on how influenced they are by emotional and superficial factors. This is important to keep in mind, as it can affect the amount of equity you can use to build your portfolio, as happened to me with my very first property.

Your credit file

Your credit history and rating can make or break a property transaction, so it's important to stay on top of it. Many investors don't realise just how much information goes into their file and the huge impact it can have on their efforts to obtain finance over their lifetime. Every time a bank or lender processes an application for finance, they will run a credit enquiry to check your credit history, and this will be recorded on the file. This record also includes applications for any line of credit, such as personal loans, car finance, a phone contract or furniture for your home. Your credit file also records whether you make your repayments on time, your existing debts and whether or not any applications have been rejected.

Based on your credit history, you are assigned a credit score that can range between 200 and 1200. This is then placed on a five-point scale ranging from excellent to below average. The average Australian sits at around 550.

Even if your credit score is quite good, multiple enquiries made on your file by banks and lenders in a short space of time tend not to be looked on favourably. For instance, despite having a credit score of 765, which is considered to be very good, I have been declined for a loan for this reason. This is why it is important to consider whether it is necessary to submit an application with a bank when seeking a valuation on your property.

You can improve your credit score by always paying your bills on time and being mindful of how these enquiries can affect it. Your credit history is a vital yet often overlooked aspect of investing in property, and a good credit score is your golden ticket to obtaining finance.

If you are serious about investing, I highly recommend paying for a subscription to a credit reporting agency such as Equifax. This will give you easy access to your file, which will allow you to monitor your history and score, and to determine areas in which you could improve.

Structuring your portfolio

There are a number of ways in which you can purchase property and structure your portfolio, some more advantageous than others in terms of finance.

Individual purchase

An individual person buys and owns the property, and is 100 per cent liable for the debt held against the property by the lender. This is the simplest and most common form of property ownership.

Joint-name purchasing

The property is purchased under two or more individuals' names. This is often done by couples, family members, friends or investing partners, as discussed in chapter 9. To recap, the disadvantage of this when investing is that if one person in the partnership wants to purchase another property, the bank will attribute the total amount owing on the existing property as their liability. In other words, even though you technically own half of the property's debt, in the bank's eyes you own and are responsible for all of it. This can restrict your borrowing capacity, and therefore your investing capabilities.

Purchasing in a trust

I started buying properties through trust structures when I already had 11 properties in my name. I don't recommend beginner investors buy through a trust for several reasons:

- It can be harder to obtain finance through a trust due to banking policies.

- It's expensive to set up.

- You generally have to pay more land tax.

Whether and when to purchase properties through a trust depends on many variables relating to your financial position. The benefits, of course, are that trusts provide asset protection and income distribution, which are both very valuable, but it gets complex. Before setting up a trust I always recommend speaking with experienced property investors and a qualified tax accountant who has personal property investment experience to give you advice.

Purchasing under a business name

This can be an option for business owners. Under this structure, though, it can be more difficult to obtain finance, depending on how long the business has been trading for, as well as on the income of the business itself. Further, the LVRs are usually much higher, at around 70 to 80 per cent, meaning you will need a larger deposit. Work out what structure is going to work best for your situation.

Negative gearing

Lots of people invest in property for the tax breaks and depreciation benefits. There are some advantages to this strategy, but it's not one I necessarily recommend.

Negative gearing is a strategy used by investors to buy a rental property expecting the gross income generated to be less than the costs of owning and managing the investment. These costs include depreciation and interest charged on the loan, but not principal repayments. These losses are then used as tax breaks. Essentially, you are losing money to claim a portion of it back.

Negative gearing arrangements offer a form of financial leverage. Investors depend on the tax benefits (if any) and the capital gain on the investment (when it is eventually disposed of) exceeding the accumulated losses of holding the investment. It is a *growth* strategy.

For me, it makes more sense to build your portfolio from a *cash flow positive* or at least *cash flow neutral* position. I believe it's acceptable to have a few negatively geared properties in a large portfolio with many positively geared ones, because based on their instant equity position or future growth potential they could be well worth it, but these have to be balanced with cash-flow-positive properties to help lighten their burden. It is also important to have a balancing strategy in place in case something goes wrong, such as an extended period of vacancy.

The truth about financial advisers

If you want to learn about fitness and body building, who would you prefer to learn from? A professor who has studied everything in the world about it, but has never lifted a weight in his life, or Arnold Schwarzenegger? The answer is a no-brainer, but in my experience, going to a financial adviser for advice can be a bit like going to the professor who has never lifted a weight. Financial advisers may have the theoretical knowledge and book smarts, but most have little direct experience of investing.

To me it makes sense to check a person's practical experience before their formal qualifications. I'd rather listen to a self-made millionaire with no degrees than a person with a handful of degrees but no personal wealth-creation experience. On this subject, if you haven't yet read Robert Kiyosaki's *Rich Dad, Poor Dad*, I strongly recommend it.

The other issue to keep in mind about financial advisers is that they will sometimes receive a commission from persuading you to invest in a particular product, in which case they are not giving you honest, independent advice. For example, many financial advisers encourage investors to buy property 'off the plan', because they get a hefty commission from the developer. These types of properties are usually way overpriced, and I've seen them send unwary investors into bankruptcy.

This kind of unethical behaviour was identified back in 2009 by the Australian Securities and Investments Commission (ASIC), and more was uncovered by the banking royal commission in 2017, which also showed that the general public often don't believe that banks or financial advisers have their clients' best interest in mind. So, given that most of them have little or no personal experience as investors, and what's more, they are getting commissions to sell you products or properties that are overpriced, why would you go to one for help?

The banking royal commission led to new legislation addressing what it means to be an 'independent financial adviser', which basically means that they can't receive any commissions or other benefits for recommending investment products, but there are still very few financial planners who actually meet this new definition of 'independent'.

If you do decide to consult a financial adviser, I recommend asking them these questions before you commit to anything.

- What personal experience do you have with creating wealth? (I recommend expressing this one in a friendly way, as it can sound rather forward.)

- How long have you been a financial adviser, and do you personally own shares or investment properties like the ones you recommend? (This is basically asking, do you practise what you preach?) Do you, in other words, have first-hand experience?

For me it's a no-brainer. Always learn from someone who has done it before with proven results!

Monitoring your portfolio

When investing in property, it is vital to keep a regular eye on your properties' performance. This involves checking every day, week and month to see what is selling in the areas around your investments and noting comparable sales. If comparable properties are selling for higher than your original purchase price, you may have new equity available.

For example, imagine you have purchased a property for $300000. In one year's time, if you notice that other properties of similar size, with a comparable number of bedrooms and bathrooms and car spaces and similar layout and overall presentation, are selling for $350000, then the odds are your property could be revalued at that same amount. Banks consider the current market conditions and comparable sales and overall presentation when calculating their valuations.

By monitoring the properties in your portfolio carefully, you can identify the best opportunities to achieve strong valuations and release equity to use for your next property. This is crucial if you want to reach the top 0.1 per cent of property investors.

CHAPTER 11
The deposit

Before you can begin your investment journey, you need the money for the first deposit and closing costs. Some people ask me if they can buy a house without savings. The answer, technically, is yes, though I wouldn't recommend it. Here are a couple of options.

Option 1: Personal loan

You can use a personal loan as the deposit, but it's a risky move. To be able to service a personal loan and a mortgage (and to get both approved!) you need a high income, little or no other debt, a clear credit history and usually at least some savings. If you meet these criteria, you should easily be able to save for a deposit! So I recommend you use your high income wisely, save as much as you can and pay for the deposit and closing costs yourself.

Option 2: Guarantor loan

If you are concerned about being able to save enough for a deposit, you could consider securing a guarantor loan. This means someone else—usually parents—guarantees your mortgage with their own house.

Guarantor loans are useful because:

- a deposit is not required to get the mortgage

- LMI is not required

- the interest rates are competitive

- you can borrow the money for the closing costs on top of the purchase price, saving thousands.

Guarantor loans are risky because if you fail to meet the mortgage repayments, the bank could claim possession of your guarantor's house and sell it to get back the money they lent to you. This is a big ask of your parents, so consider it only if you are 100 per cent confident that situation will never arise.

To be accepted, your guarantor must have a property in Australia that has equity to cover you, and they must be working—it's rare for lenders to accept retired guarantors. A guarantor will usually be your parents, but close relatives can be accepted too.

Option 3: Using equity from a property you already own

You may be able to use equity from a property you already own by having the property revalued. Before doing this you can get a rough idea of how much your property is worth by researching what prices similar properties in your area have recently sold for. This will help you determine if your property's value has increased enough to be worth getting a formal valuation, so you can then release equity and use it for the deposit for your next purchase. For example, let's say the property is valued at $500 000 and the current loan is sitting at $300000. The banks will usually lend you 80 per cent of the property value (80 per cent of $500000 = $400000). Deduct the loan amount, and you have $100000 of equity!

Now you can refinance and draw out the $100000 equity in cash. The loan on this property will increase from $300000 to $400000, but it gives you an instant cash injection to purchase more. You could use that $100000 as two deposits of $50000 each and go out and buy two more properties worth $350000, each with 10 per cent deposits ($35000 + $15000 closing costs). The value of your property portfolio has just grown $500000 to $1.2 million!

Some people hesitate to do this because they're concerned about increasing the loan and the mortgage repayments. I understand this, but if you are choosing a long-term wealth-creation strategy, it is far more powerful to use this equity to purchase two more properties. The cash flow and capital growth gained by these extra properties over the next 20 to 50 years far outweighs the cost of the increase in mortgage repayments (which can be paid by the rental income from the property or, worst case, by one of the new properties you purchased using that capital).

In 2019 I used equity from a property I owned in western Sydney for the deposit for a dual-occupancy property in Brisbane. The loan for the western Sydney property was $640000, and I had a new bank valuation come in at $950000. I decided to increase the mortgage on that property to 80 per cent of this new valuation and was able to extract $120000. To run you through the numbers:

$$20\% \text{ of } \$950\,000 = \$190\,000$$

$$\$950\,000 - \$190\,000 = \$760\,000$$

$$\$760\,000 - \$640\,000 = \$120\,000$$

I could have gone further and taken the western Sydney property up to a 90 per cent LVR, which would have released $215000 (minus the LMI fee that I would have had to pay, which would probably have been between $10000 and $20000).

I now had $120000 for a deposit and closing costs. I found a dual-occupancy property 30 minutes from Brisbane's CBD that looked promising. The owner had originally bought it off the plan from a house and land developer, who sold them on the depreciation and tax benefits (as I've noted, these are almost always overpriced). He'd paid $190000 for the land and roughly $330000 for the build, a total of almost $520000! The property was on a large block, with a three-bedroom property on one side and a two-bedroom property on the other. The two properties were under one roof with a common wall down the middle, and the combined rent was $570 per week. I was able to purchase it at an urgent price reduction for only $410000, which gave me a gross yield of 7.22 per cent.

Table 11.1 shows how the numbers stacked up.

One of my first duplex properties, boasting two income streams

Table 11.1: calculations for the second duplex I bought in 2020

Estimated expenses	Weekly ($)	Monthly ($)	Annually ($)
Council rates	32.69	141.67	1700.00
Strata fees inc. building insurance	–	–	–
Water rates	26.92	116.67	1400.00
Building insurance	15.38	66.67	800.00
Management fees	34.62	150.00	1800.00
Repayments 2.75% interest only	192.31	833.33	10000.00
Landlord insurance	7.69	33.33	400.00
Estimated totals	**309.62**	**1341.67**	**16100.00**
Income comparables			
Lower rent	570.00	2470.00	29640.00
Higher rent	620.00	2686.67	32240.00
Estimated cash flow before tax			
Lower rent	260.38	1128.33	13540.00
Higher rent	310.38	1345.00	16140.00

Overall this property brought in $13000 of passive income a year from day one. On top of this it was also only four years old, so it had major depreciation tax benefits. Depreciation is a massive bonus to get tax refunds and ultimately grow your property portfolio and wealth much faster. Buying newish properties like this one at a good price is always *far* better than buying off the plan, though.

I was really happy with this property purchase, as it met my three key criteria:

1. **Growth potential.** With a capital city location (within 30 minutes' drive of Brisbane's CBD), it had huge future growth potential.

2. **Cash flow.** This property had great cash flow! That isn't true of all my investments. It's important to remember that all properties will have pros and cons, so there's no point waiting for the perfect one. I've seen hundreds of would-be investors miss the boat entirely because they were forever 'keeping their options open' and waiting for the 'best', passing up many amazing opportunities because of analysis paralysis.

3. **Below market value.** The question to ask: is this property good value? Below market value does *not* mean buying it below the asking price. It means buying it at a price significantly lower than comparable properties nearby have recently sold for.

Choosing the deposit

For this dual-occupancy property I chose to pay a 10 per cent deposit along with the LMI to save capital. This is how the numbers broke down:

10% deposit	$41 000
Stamp duty	$13 000
Legal fees and pest & building report	$2000
Miscellaneous buffer expenses / LMI	$6000
Total rough figure	**$62 000**

Here are the numbers if I had chosen to pay a 20 per cent deposit:

20% deposit	$81 000
Stamp duty	$13 000
Legal fees and pest & building report	$2000
Miscellaneous buffer expenses	$2000
Total rough figure	**$98 000**

Out of the 30+ investment properties I have personally bought, I have sometimes chosen 10 per cent deposits, 20 per cent deposits and even 40 per cent deposits. If I was starting out again, I would choose smaller deposits first to stretch my initial savings, because at the end of the day, the LMI can be tax deductible and is calculated from the purchase price, so the lower the purchase price, the lower the LMI fee.

My tips for saving for a deposit

Saving for a deposit requires discipline. You've got to connect to your *why* and to want that goal badly enough that you're willing to sacrifice some of the comforts you currently enjoy. Here are my seven tips to help get you there.

1. Review your expenses

Review the spreadsheet you created outlining your current financial position. Look at every single expense item to get clear on where every dollar goes. Then assess how much of that is pure necessity? Can any of it be cut back? What one or two expenses bring you such joy that to keep them you're happy to cut other non-essentials? Maybe you decide that eating out once a week is something you so look forward to that you're willing to forgo buying any new clothes this year. (Don't most of us have clothes we never get around to wearing anyway?)

2. Review your income

How much do you make? How can you increase it? Can you ask for a pay rise or apply for a similar job with a higher salary? Can you pick up a second job one day a week? If you do that second job for a whole year, how much more in savings will you have at the end of the year?

3. Review your debt

Do you have any debts? Perhaps a car loan or credit card debt? Whatever it is, pay it off as quickly as you can and vow that in future you will not go into debt for anything other than a property. I recommend not even having a credit card! When the temptation is right there, it's much harder to resist. If you don't have a credit card, you won't have any credit card debt. (If you have a credit card you're paying off, get a debit card and leave your credit card in a drawer at home. Keep it until it's paid off, then enjoy cutting it up and throwing it away!)

4. Automate your savings

Do you have a savings account? If not, open one. And just as you have set up an automatic payment to pay off a credit card or to pay your rent, set up an automatic savings transfer. The day your pay cheque lands, immediately transfer your savings out. (If you've done the spreadsheet, you'll already know what your monthly savings figure is.)

5. Delay gratification

Now is the time for you to go all out! Focus on finding cheap or free ways to have fun, such as staying home and making your own popcorn rather than going to the movies, or bringing leftovers for lunch the next day. Find ways to reduce every single expense you can. Control those impulses. Remember your end goal.

6. Plan meals

One of the biggest expenses that can get out of control is eating out. Like most Australians, you probably love eating out! But it costs a lot, so much more than cooking yourself. Find new recipes online and try them out. Build a repertoire of dishes you love. Spend 10 minutes on Sunday planning the meals for the week before you go grocery shopping, and stick to the plan. You'll save heaps of money—and enjoy the fruits of your labour!

7. Keep thinking abundantly

Some people, when they save, can get into a poverty mindset. Don't let your savings measures get you into that trap. Remember, you're doing this to buy an *investment property!* How sweet is that? It's epic! You're going to be so happy with yourself in five, ten, 50 years' time. So focus on the positives. Focus on the fact that you're being smart with your money. You're being thoughtful and disciplined. Dream about your future life when you reach your property goal. Dream about the extravagant things you'll be able to do then. Keep your mindset one of abundance and focus.

Delayed gratification

I want to discuss this point in more detail. It's not a topic that many property investment books talk about, yet it's crucial if you want to become financially free in the future. It means sacrificing something you want now in order to be smart with your money, so you can enjoy financial freedom later on. It means resisting a smaller but more immediate desire in order to receive a larger or more enduring reward later.

Now, I happen to love old-school Ford Mustangs, the styles you see in the movies, like the 1967 GT500 Shelby Mustang in *Gone in 60 Seconds* and the 1969 Mach 1 in *John Wick*.

When I had 12 properties I had the money in my bank account (from equity and cash flow) to buy both these cars. Still I delayed gratification. I finally bought a Mustang when I had more than 20 investment properties, worth more than $7 million. What's more, I believe these cars will grow in value over time, rather than depreciating like most modern cars.

You should enjoy life now, but you also need to prepare for the future. You don't want to reach your fifties and find you can't do anything because you blew all your money when you were younger.

Buying nice things is all about the numbers. How much cash/ equity do you have in the bank, and can you justify setting back your long-term financial goals for that new car?

I was once asked by a close friend who loves Ferraris, 'How much money would you need in the bank before you spent $500 000 on buying a Ferrari outright?' My answer was a minimum of $10 million cash. He was horrified.

For me, it's a percentage game. If your net worth is only $2 million, should you really consider spending a quarter of that on a ridiculously expensive item that quickly depreciates in value like a Ferrari? It's the dumbest thing I can imagine. If I really had to have that Ferrari, I would instead invest the $2 million wisely, make $20 million or more (over many years) and only then, once I had a good safety buffer, think about buying it.

Here's my 1969 Ford Mustang Mach 1 Fast Back.

Once you hit a long-term goal, be sure to spoil yourself!

The second car I bought (once I had a property portfolio worth $8 million) was a huge family car—a brand-new Toyota Sahara 200 series.

Build up your portfolio before spending big on yourself—let the property assets pay for the liabilities.

When you delay gratification and invest wisely for a decade, you are also in a financial position to help those you love. Most people couldn't imagine being able to afford to buy a house in a good but expensive suburb for their mother. But that's one of the many benefits of having been frugal, saving and investing wisely.

Self-managed super fund (SMSF)

If you're keen to start investing but don't have a deposit saved, but you do have money in your super account, consider setting up as a self-managed super fund (SMSF). That way you can use the money in your super account as the deposit! It does come with a lot of extra paperwork and compliance, but with the right team I believe it's a viable option for everyone. Property investors can offload almost all the paperwork to tax accountants and property managers to handle, but finding good professionals to work with, of course, requires the right prior knowledge and thorough investigation.

It's essential you find an accountant who has personal property investing experience. At the very least, ask them how many clients they have with five, ten or 15+ properties, and to give you a few examples of obstacles they helped their clients overcome. I've found that most accountants don't have this experience. Every week I have a client telling me their accountant said it wasn't worth buying property through their SMSF, or that they needed a minimum of $250 000 in super. This is incorrect and simply demonstrates these accountants' lack of experience. You need to hunt for an accountant with lots of property buying experience.

SMSF loans are different in that the lowest deposit you can put down on a loan through a SMSF is 20 per cent, and right now only three banks will accept this LVR:

- Latrobe Financial
- Liberty Financial
- Granite Financial.

Let's say you have $100000 in super. You can choose to set up an SMSF and roll that money into it, and use the $100000 as a deposit to buy a $400000 property ($80000 to cover the 20 per cent deposit and the remaining $20000 to cover the closing costs).

Another difference with owning property through an SMSF is the interest rates, which are much higher compared with buying a property in your name. This means the cash flow of the property will be lower, but it's still possible to get it to be neutrally or even positively geared.

I bought my first property through my SMSF in late 2017. At the time I was stuck with serviceability; I couldn't buy another property in my own name! It's very common with large property portfolios that the banks become more and more cautious. I wanted to continue growing my portfolio, so I looked into other ways I could do so and decided to set up an SMSF. At the time I had only $50000 in superannuation, and no accountant, financial planner or SMSF expert I spoke with would take me seriously. They kept insisting I didn't have enough in super. 'You need a minimum of $200000 in your SMSF to qualify for a loan.'

But, despite being knocked back more than a dozen times, three months later I was able to purchase a property. I found it through a real estate connection I had made over the years. It was off market for only $153000 and was being rented out for $290 a week (a 10.02 per cent gross yield!). And it was in a growing, regentrified area only a 22-minute drive to the heart of Brisbane's CBD.

Table 11.2 (overleaf) shows how the numbers stacked up.

Table 11.2: calculations for my first SMSF property purchase in 2017

Estimated expenses	Weekly ($)	Monthly ($)	Annually ($)
Council rates	30.77	133.33	1600.00
Strata fees inc. building insurance	23.08	100.00	1200.00
Water rates	23.08	100.00	1200.00
Building insurance	–	–	–
Management fees	19.23	83.33	1000.00
Mortgage repayments (SMSF rate)	151.92	658.33	7900.00
Landlord insurance	6.15	26.67	320.00
Estimated totals	**254.23**	**1101.67**	**13220.00**
Income comparables			
Lower rent	290.00	1256.67	15080.00
Higher rent	300.00	1300.00	15600.00
Estimated cash flow before tax			
Lower rent	35.77	155.00	1860.00
Higher rent	45.77	198.33	2380.00

The mortgage is principal and interest with an interest rate of 5.2 per cent (which is high), but overall the property is still self-sufficient. The numbers looked like this:

20% deposit	$30600
Stamp duty	$4000
Legal fees and pest & building report	$2000
Miscellaneous buffer expenses	$2000
Total rough figure	**$38000**

My first SMSF purchase

This property was the first of five I have now bought through my SMSF.

CLIENT EXAMPLES

I really want to inspire you. You can do this. You can invest in property, build a portfolio and retire early. It's genuinely possible. Here are two property purchase examples from a couple of clients of mine.

James

James contacted me in 2020. He wanted to buy his first property and begin growing a property portfolio to create long-term wealth. His end goal was to create a passive income of $60 000 to $100 000 a year that he could live off.

(continued)

James was 27, lived in western Sydney and worked as a printer technician / courier. His initial savings were roughly $60000. Within 12 months he bought three properties.

His first property was a $288000 four-bed, two-bath, two-car garage within 30 minutes of the Brisbane CBD. (The owner had bought it off the plan in 2012 and paid $400000 for it!) The rent was $360 a week, giving a yield of 6.5 per cent. It was in a growth location and bought for $40000 under market value. Twelve months later it was valued at $380000.

Table 11.3 gives a breakdown of the numbers for this property.

James's first investment property

Table 11.3: calculations for James's property

Estimated expenses	Weekly ($)	Monthly ($)	Annually ($)
Council rates	28.85	125.00	1500.00
Strata fees inc. building insurance	–	–	–
Water rates	26.92	116.67	1400.00
Building insurance	15.38	66.67	800.00
Management fees	21.15	91.67	1100.00
Repayments 2.75 % interest only	157.69	683.33	8200.00
Landlord insurance	5.77	25.00	300.00
Estimated totals	**255.77**	**1108.33**	**13300.00**
Income comparables			
Lower rent	340.00	1473.33	17680.00
Higher rent	360.00	1560.00	18720.00
Estimated cash flow before tax			
Lower rent	84.23	365.00	4380.00
Higher rent	104.23	451.67	5420.00

Alex and Danielle

In late 2019, Alex and Danielle contacted me for help buying their next investment property (they already owned one in Victoria, where they lived). Alex and Danielle were in their mid-thirties, lived in Melbourne and worked in corporate for middle incomes. Alex had been researching different ways of investing their money for a few years, because he'd realised that if they didn't invest he would have to work until he was 70 and would still not have much left over for retirement.

So they were looking for a better strategy. They wanted properties that had higher yields and growth, and that could be bought below market value. Over the next 12 months, through 2020, they bought four properties.

They bought their fifth investment property in Brisbane for $219 000 on a 10 per cent deposit. The comparable market price was $250 000. It was an urgent distress sale during COVID.

The owner had bought this townhouse off the plan five years before for $340 000 (certainly overpaying). It drew a rent of $360 a week, giving a yield of 8.56 per cent. The new valuation was $280 000.

Table 11.4 shows how the figures stacked up.

Here's how Alex described their experience:

'The more we researched investing options, the more convinced we became that real estate was the best option; it's what I felt most comfortable doing to grow our wealth. I started reading investment books, like Robert Kiyosaki's *Rich Dad, Poor Dad* and Scott Pape's *The Barefoot Investor*, and I also listened to podcasts such as *Property Investory*, which introduced me to the idea of using a buyer's agent.

I wanted to work with someone who had a substantial property portfolio themselves, who could teach me how they were able to build a property portfolio that

Table 11.4: calculations for Alex and Danielle's Brisbane townhouse

Estimated expenses	Weekly ($)	Monthly ($)	Annually ($)
Council rates	28.85	125.00	1500.00
Strata fees inc. building insurance	69.23	300.00	3600
Water rates	23.08	100.00	1200.00
Building insurance	–	–	–
Management fees	21.15	91.67	1100.00
Estimated mortgage repayments	103.85	450.00	5400.00
Landlord insurance	5.77	25.00	300.00
Estimated totals	**251.92**	**1091.67**	**13100.00**

Income comparables			
Lower rent	330.00	1430.00	17160.00
Higher rent	360.00	1560.00	32240.00

Estimated cash flow before tax			
Lower rent	78.08	338.33	4060.00
Higher rent	108.08	468.33	5620.00

was cash flow positive and gaining in capital growth. Property investment can seem like a big commitment. You're dealing with large sums of money, so having someone to help us understand the process, teach

(continued)

us what to look out for in property contracts, and
be on our side to find excellent deals and negotiate
great prices so we were making money on the way
in, made the experience so much more fortunate.
Dilleen Property is more than Eddie. He has a team
who worked together with us throughout the process,
including mortgage brokers, solicitors, building
and pest inspectors, and property managers. This
made investing interstate possible, and the ongoing
management of the properties seamless. We intend
to continue to build our property portfolio and
leverage off the properties we have to keep building
our wealth.'

CHAPTER 12
How to find a property

When you're starting out it's hard not to fret about whether you're buying at the right time or getting a good deal on the property you're hoping to invest in. I started by researching many different areas so I could narrow down which areas I wanted to buy in. I then spent a lot of time, on the ground and online, learning all I could about the area, amenities, public transport, schools and what properties in the area were selling for.

If I were starting all over again now, I would zoom out to look at Australia as a whole. What most people do when they first start is to look at areas they know. But this is so limiting! When investing, you need to take the emotion out of it. You live in Sydney? Who cares? You think Melbourne is a cool city? So what. All that matters is finding a good property. So zoom out. Consider every state. How is the property market in WA at the moment? South Australia? Queensland? Tasmania? ACT? Northern Territory? Victoria and NSW? Investigate the market in each state. What is the average price of a metro property? Which state is seeing or about to see the most growth?

You can find a lot of this information for free online. Do the research, listen to podcasts and YouTube channels and read this book to the end! A lot of the time, and now especially, I buy in the Brisbane or the greater Queensland market. But I also like buying in Sydney.

Once you decide on a state, you need to focus in on an area within the state.

City vs regional areas

There is a big difference between buying in a regional area and in a metro area. The regional property market often moves at a different pace, though it can be great for long-term investment. Often regional towns will offer a higher rental yield than a standard house near a major city, but it is more difficult to choose a good location, and therefore it's a riskier investment path. I, personally, have no properties in regional areas.

If you do want to invest regionally, do your research to find out about infrastructure plans in the area. Is a hospital set to be built there soon? Or a new office building / factory that will bring more jobs to the area? What existing infrastructure is there already? If the town you're looking at relies on one source for jobs — a mine, for example — then it's a risky move. If the mine closes or the power station shuts down, the value of your property will plummet and be unlikely to bounce back any time soon, if ever.

To invest in the regions, you need to be especially thorough with your research. Really dive into the data. What are the auction clearance rates? (Auction clearance rates for each town or suburb, available online, will tell you how many of the houses that went to auction were sold at auction.) When auction clearance rates are high — 80 per cent and above — it means the market is hot.

Lower clearance rates mean the market is steadier and there's more opportunity to find a bargain. Auction clearance rates usually don't dip too low, because if the real estate agents in that suburb aren't getting good results, they'll stop selling through auctions. How long do properties take to sell? What are the rental yields, the vacancy rates and the average time needed to get a property tenanted?

My preferred strategy is to invest in metro areas. When you take the emotion out and just look at the numbers, it's always possible to find properties quite close to a major city that have higher rental yields than regional properties.

Why I love metro properties

I love properties located in metro areas because the infrastructure has already been built. There are good hospitals, shops, schools, universities and train stations. All this makes the area much more liveable. Metro is also more desirable because it's closer to where most people work. I like that there's an established large population: most Australian cities have a population of at least one or two million people, and they continue to grow.

If you've chosen a capital city, can you buy 10 kilometres out or do you have to buy 30 kilometres out? Once you figure this out, start visiting the areas you're interested in. Attend open houses. Look at what properties are selling for now and what they've sold for in the past.

When looking for properties I also try to look forward into the future, based on interest rates, location, proximity to the CBD, the stage the current property market is at and population growth. I think, *Could this property be worth 30 to 50 per cent or even 100 per cent more in the next seven, ten or 15 years? Is that feasible, based on the rent, average wages in the area, location and inflation rate (past and present)?*

An awesome example!

Many investors wait for economic downturns, when they can pick up the best bargains for stocks and real estate. Warren Buffett, one of the world's best investors, famously advised, 'Be fearful when others are greedy and greedy when others are fearful.' Take massive investing action when others are fearful, as the money is made in the slumps and lows.

During 2020 I was able to pick up many great properties when others were too scared of the economic impacts of COVID-19 to take action. I found this one in Brisbane. The seller was nearing retirement and needed to get rid of it quickly, so an urgent auction was set.

A real estate agent I had bought many properties from in the past called and alerted me to the situation a couple days before the auction, so I had the chance to do a little research beforehand, but much of it fell into a frantic half hour before the auction. It was a Saturday afternoon so I ran to the office and jumped on the computer. I'd pulled up RP Data reports, checked comparable sales and all the usual due diligence. I'd also called my mortgage broker, who did two desktop bank valuations through Westpac and NAB, which came back at $390000 and $370000.

The property was a house with an attached granny flat on a 950 square metre block roughly 30 minutes' drive from the heart of Brisbane's CBD. I'd researched rentals in the area and found I could rent the house for somewhere between $290 and $320 a week, and rent the granny flat for between $250 and $300 a week. Alternatively, I could rent the whole property to a large family for around $500 a week.

RP Data told me that the council valued the land itself at roughly $250000 (in different states in Australia some councils will value the land of a property annually, making this available through RP Data). New vacant blocks of about half the size close by were being sold individually for $220 000 to $280 000!

The fact that this property was on a 950 square metre block really stood out for me. I quickly completed the paperwork for bidding on a property over the phone (signing an authority form and a disclosure statement, emailing through identification and so on). Three minutes before the auction started I called the agent (who was at the property) to give my bidding instructions. I asked how many other bidders were there, and she answered that two other bidders were there and registering.

My heart raced with nervous excitement. I tried to swallow this and just focus on the numbers. Based on my research I was prepared to pay $310 000 to buy it at auction, as it was a higher risk. I didn't have finance approved and buying at auction in Queensland makes the contract of sale 'unconditional'. This means it's not subject to a pest and building report or finance. If I won at auction there was no going back, not even if the house turned out to have structural issues or I couldn't get my finance approved. In such a case I would face a risk of legal action.

Over the phone I heard the auctioneer welcome those present and explain the standard terms under which the auction would be carried out. Then it began. The auctioneer asked for an opening bid, and the usual dead silence descended. After 30 seconds I jumped in with $280 000. Seconds later another bidder offered $285 000, and another $290 000, then I offered $295 000. And there it ended. The agent told me I was the only one left and it was between me and the owner to try to come to an agreement because the reserve hadn't been met. If it didn't sell that day, they would present all offers to the owner right away.

I knew that if I let it go and it ceased to be unconditional, chances are the property would go for much more—probably $330 000 or even as much as $350000 or more. So I played hardball with the seller until we ended up at $309000. I pushed for a 90-day settlement so I would have more time to get finance approved (which always takes longer when you have a substantial property portfolio).

A rent of $520 a week (worst case) or $620 a week (best case) would produce a gross yield of 8.41 per cent or 10.4 per cent.

Table 12.1 shows how the numbers stacked up.

Table 12.1: calculations for the 2020 house and granny flat purchase

Estimated expenses	Weekly ($)	Monthly ($)	Annually ($)
Council rates	30.77	133.33	1600.00
Strata fees inc. building insurance	–	–	–
Water rates	25.00	108.33	1300.00
Building insurance	15.38	66.67	800.00
Management fees	36.54	158.33	1900.00
Mortgage repayments (current interest rate)	136.54	591.67	7100.00
Landlord insurance	10.58	45.83	550.00
Estimated totals	**254.81**	**1104.17**	**13250.00**
Income comparables			
Lower rent	520.00	2253.33	27040.00
Higher rent	620.00	2686.67	32240.00
Estimated cash flow before tax			
Lower rent	265.19	1149.17	13790.00
Higher rent	365.19	1582.50	18990.00

House and granny flat – one of my favourite property purchases to date

The property was bought below market value (at roughly 20 per cent under the bank valuations, which is massive!), was cash flow positive from day one, and of course had a huge capital growth upside.

As I write this, it's been 12 months since I bought this property, and I have had multiple valuations and appraisals done. This month they came in at $550 000 to $600 000, which means it has almost doubled in 12 months! This is unreal. The market was already low because of the pandemic, but I also bought under market value, and in 2021 markets have risen rapidly. Such a great buy!

It's easy to read this and maybe think you've missed the boat, but while this property is an outlier, it's important to recognise that incredible opportunities are available *right now*. We regularly update our YouTube channel with new examples of properties that both our clients and I have bought, so check it out for inspiration and motivation.

Do your research

There are vast amounts of readily accessible data and resources online that you can use when conducting your research. Many people look no further than realestate.com or Domain to find out what's currently for sale. Once they've decided on the area they want to buy in, they check what's listed. They might filter the real estate pages from lowest to highest selling price. That's great, but it's not research. It's just looking at what's currently listed and prices the vendor is hoping to get.

You need to get a feel for what properties are worth, and you'll gain that insight by seeing what properties have sold for in the past three to six months. Go onto realestate.com or Domain, and search for properties that have sold in the same location, filtered from newest to oldest. You can set filters for what kind of property you're interested in, so if you're looking for a three-bedroom house with one bathroom, set the filters to show what these houses recently sold for.

At the beginning of my property journey I didn't understand that with online listings the agents or vendors can ask for any price they want, and they can change that asking price at any time. A lot of people who look online will see a property listed for $450000 and assume it must be worth $440000 to $450000. But it could be worth substantially less, or it could be worth more. It's all about doing the research. You need to check what properties have actually been selling for.

I know many agents. Some work for the big companies, others for small franchises, but they all have the apps on their phones through which they manage the listings. If they list a property for $450000 and it's not moving, and the owner is desperate to get rid of it, they can just jump on their phones and drop the price by $60000. Just like that. It's crazy. They can put in an inflated listing price that bears no relation to the property's actual worth.

Doing this research is called doing a comparable sales analysis or, as agents call it, a comparable market analysis (CMA). When someone first joins a real estate office, as I did when I was 19, one of the first things they're taught is how to do a CMA. Agents usually use RP Data (for 'Rich Property Data'), which is Australia's biggest and most used platform for real estate information. RP Data is a subscription product all agencies buy. It gives them access to 20 years of property data collected by CoreLogic.

The CMA is how real estate agents determine a selling price — no, it isn't just picked out of thin air! But of course some vendors ask to list a higher price to see if they can get away with it, which is why you need to do your research.

Timing

When conducting your research, you also need to consider market trends. Is the market really heated right now, with lots of buyers out there, or is it slowing down? You have possibly heard the term *property clock* thrown around in investing circles. Whether you're making your first purchase or are an experienced investor, property clocks can help you determine the best time to buy and sell your investment.

It can be difficult to know what stage of its cycle the market is in, which is where property clocks come into play. Property markets tend to go through a cycle and the timing of your purchase or sale within that cycle can make a difference of tens of thousands of dollars. A property clock is a tool that visually represents the different stages of the property market cycle. Generally, the market will go through a boom of high prices, followed by a downswing as prices fall then stabilise. This is followed by a recovery period as prices begin to rise again towards the next boom.

Using the clock analogy, when the hour hand is at 12, the property market is in a boom period when demand is outpacing supply and prices are at their peak. As the hand moves clockwise, prices begin to cool until it reaches six. At six, an oversupply of houses means the market bottoms out. As the hand continues its journey, rental prices start to improve and interest rates fall. This increases the demand for housing and prices begin to rise again until it reaches the peak of the next boom (see figure 12.1).

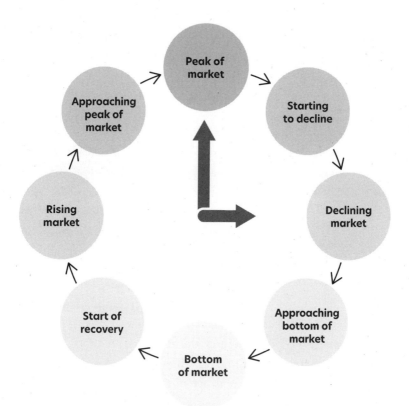

Figure 12.1: the property clock

How to use the property clock

The property clock is a great visual reference, but it also serves a practical purpose. By working out where a suburb sits on the clock, you can time the market just right to get the best value for money on your transaction. The property clock offers some confidence and reliability in predicting which regions and suburbs are ripe for investment, and can help new investors gain a better understanding of the cycle. Once you become familiar with the different periods of market performance, you will begin to notice patterns and trends that indicate where a suburb may be sitting, and use this understanding when making your next move.

Let's say, for example, you've worked out that a regional area of NSW is sitting at around 7 or 8 o'clock on the cycle. Now could be the perfect time to buy, as prices are still low and there is the potential for a substantial upswing in values before the boom period occurs. On the other hand, if the region sits at 12 o'clock, this is the worst time to buy as prices are at their absolute peak. By using the property clock, you can work out the best times to buy and sell and develop a safe and successful property investment strategy.

Working out where a region sits

Accurately predicting the 'time' on the property clock for a particular region can sometimes be easier said than done. While cycles are generally well established, they rarely follow a predictable path around the clock, and there are always variables that can change things. Factors that can affect the cycle can range from small local influences to major global events. For example, if a town's largest industry or employer experiences a downturn, which results in mass layoffs, you can expect the local market to cool. On the other hand, if national interest rates fall, this will lead to increased housing demand due to more favourable borrowing conditions, which in turn will lead to a rise in prices.

Another sign to look out for is rising prices and auction clearing rates of more than 60 per cent (although this can vary, depending on the state or area). Both indicate a rising market, while properties selling for higher than the asking price and being listed for short periods can indicate the market has reached its peak.

Limitations of the property clock

While property clocks are undoubtedly useful, like any prediction tool, they should be used with caution. There is always going to be a degree of uncertainty in real estate, and the many factors influencing market values can be neither controlled nor accurately predicted. In addition, they can cause investors to focus obsessively on short-term outlooks while forgetting about the long-term benefits of building a sustainable property portfolio. No matter what stage of the cycle you purchase in, your investment can still be very profitable in the long term if you hold onto it.

CLIENT EXAMPLE
Pete and Laura

Pete and Laura, in their late forties, lived in western Sydney. They reached out in late 2019 after seeing me on TV and checking out my social media platforms. They wanted to dip their toes in the market but didn't know how. With our help they found the process of entering the property market easy. Their objective was to buy one investment property, leave it for 12 months to see how it went, then kick on from there. Soon, though, following the service we provided them and the trust we built up, they felt comfortable accelerating their plans to take advantage of the market during COVID. They bought six properties within a year.

They had bought their first property in 2020 in the Brisbane metro area for $338 000 (under market price) on a 10 per cent deposit. The rental income was $420 a week, for a 6.4 per cent yield. Twelve months later, new valuation/

comparable sales was set at $400000+, an increase of more than $60000 in one year.

Table 12.2 gives a breakdown of the numbers for this property.

Table 12.2: calculations for Pete and Laura's first property

Estimated expenses	Weekly ($)	Monthly ($)	Annually ($)
Council rates	30.77	133.33	1600.00
Strata fees inc. building insurance	–	–	–
Water rates	26.92	116.67	1400.00
Building insurance	17.31	75.00	900.00
Management fees	23.08	100.00	1200.00
Mortgage repayments (current interest rate)	173.08	750.00	9000.00
Landlord insurance	5.77	25.00	300.00
Estimated totals	**276.92**	**1200.00**	**14400.00**
Income comparables			
Lower rent	400.00	1733.33	20800.00
Higher rent	420.00	1,820.00	21840.00
Estimated cash flow before tax			
Lower rent	123.08	533.33	6400.00
Higher rent	143.08	620.00	7440.00

(continued)

Pete and Laura's first Queensland property purchase

Factors that affect property value

When searching for a property to invest in, checking a few key factors will increase your prospects of achieving a strong return on your investment and ensure your property remains desirable to buyers in future.

Location

Location, location, location! It's an old cliché, but it's still true. The location of a property is the single most determinative factor affecting its value. Here are some questions to consider when assessing location:

- Is it close to the city centre?

- Is it close to public transport, shops, schools and restaurants?

- Does the suburb have a good reputation?

- Is it close to parks and recreation facilities?

Supply and demand

If demand exceeds supply in a market, property prices will increase. This is because there are more people looking for a smaller number of properties and the competition to score a home drives prices upwards.

Interest rates

Interest rate cuts and hikes by the Reserve Bank also impact on house prices. For example, if the Reserve Bank raises the official cash rate, the other banks and lenders will usually follow suit with higher loan rates. This will drive up the price of monthly mortgage repayments, which can have a huge impact on property affordability. When this happens, there's less competition in the real estate market and prices will drop. Conversely, an interest rate cut can drive prices, as it becomes more affordable to buy and competition increases.

Economic outlook

The overall performance of the economy also has a strong impact on the property market. If the economy is experiencing robust growth, high employment rates and good labour conditions, more people can afford to purchase a property, which leads to higher prices. Again, this is reversed if the economy starts to slow.

Property market performance

The local market performance will affect how much your property is worth. If there's little demand for properties in your neighbourhood and properties are selling for well below their worth, expect your values to fall as well.

Population and demographics

The more people who want to live in a suburb, the greater the demand for properties in that suburb. At the same time, the type of people living in the area will also influence property values. For example, if young families are the dominant demographic group in the area, multi-bedroom houses will be more sought after than small apartments.

Size and facilities

The features and overall size of a property will also influence its worth. The number of bedrooms and bathrooms, as well as features such as garages, swimming pools and balconies, will impact a property's value. Another crucial feature, particularly in metro areas, is adequate parking.

Aesthetics

The street appeal of a property can greatly influence a potential buyer's interest and therefore the value of a property. Internal functionality and styling is equally important.

Renovation potential

The potential to add value with simple renovations is important to both home buyers and investors. Scope to improve and personalise a property will make it a more attractive option and increase the potential resale value.

Investment potential

The two key factors that most obviously affect the value of investment properties are the expected rental and the potential for capital growth.

There are a few other key points to consider as well:

- **Low recent growth.** Avoid buying at the peak of an area's growth cycle.

- **Low stock on market (SOM%).** A low SOM% reflects strong demand and good buyer sentiment for the area. Avoid buying in locations where there is an oversupply of properties, as this may inhibit future growth.

- **Low vacancy rate.** Suburbs with a low vacancy rate are experiencing a shortage of available rental properties to meet demand and can therefore fetch higher rental prices.

- **High rental yield.** Suburbs with a high rental yield compared with the national average indicate good value for money, with strong potential for future capital growth.

- **Forecast demand and supply.** The presence of large-scale investment in infrastructure can indicate a projected increase in population for an area. On the other hand, a large number of residential building approvals or apartment-building projects can possibly indicate a future oversupply, meaning you will be competing with other investors.

Keeping these factors in mind when researching an area or property to invest in will help you make the best use of your money. You need to consider all the good and bad aspects of a property before deciding to pursue it.

A distressed sale

When a house needs to sell quickly, you can almost guarantee getting a better price. Perhaps the sellers need the money urgently, so they'll be willing to settle on a lower figure to get the sale done. Or perhaps it's a separation sale, and a subsidiary is involved, and again, they just want to get the house sold as quickly as possible. They might want to settle within 30 days. If so, the price will reflect that. The agent will tell people what they need to do to ensure a quick sale, and the biggest lever they can pull is dropping the price.

How a property gets listed

I want to explain a little about how properties get listed for sale online, to give you some insight into what happens behind the scenes.

A potential seller's first move is to choose a real estate agent in the area where the property is located. About 95 per cent of people in Australia will use a licensed real estate agent to sell their property, rather than trying to sell it themselves through various 'for sale by owner' sales platforms.

The agent will then conduct an appraisal. Usually they'll go out and inspect the property in person (though sometimes, depending on location, they won't even do that). They'll conduct a CMA by running valuation estimate reports on RP Data and other platforms to show recent comparable sales in the area. This data will give the agent a rough 'range of value'. They will then recommend to the seller how to list the property for sale. For example, they may suggest 'offers over $400,000' or 'asking price $460,000', or simply '$410,000 to $460,000'.

How an agent recommends the listing price and ultimately what the property is worth depends on many factors, among the biggest being the timing and market conditions. If it's an urgent sale, the agent will recommend a lower price to get the deal done quickly.

The agent will also recommend whether the house be sold at auction or be open to offers. This is decided based on what is working well in that suburb at that time—when the market is hot, agents love selling at auction because the sale is unconditional, ensuring a quicker sale. However, if the market is not strong enough to ensure a good outcome at auction, the agent will advise the vendor to be open to offers.

Finding off-market properties

Off-market properties are not advertised on platforms such as realestate.com.au and Domain. The ability to find off-market properties confers a massive advantage that other buyers don't have. But there's no cheat sheet for it; there's no 'log into this website to get access to all the off-market bargains'. Sadly, it just doesn't work like that. It takes leg work. During the years in which I bought my first 15, I actively built relationships with dozens of real estate agents, which later helped me find multiple off-market properties.

A real estate agent's job is to move property from one owner to another, and in my experience most don't care at all about who buys it. All they care about is that the property is sold, the seller and buyer achieve the result of exchanging the property, and the agent is paid their commission. Of course, some are more conscientious and caring than others. Over the years I have met some amazing real estate agents, and some horrible ones too, but overall they just want results, with that sold sticker slapped up on the board.

In the beginning I had no connections, so I had to start at the bottom like everyone else, calling the agents with listings I'd seen online on realestate.com and Domain. Calling hundreds of agents about properties they had listed over the years is hard work. Finding quality properties to invest in is a full-time job. I'm guilty of making it sound easy, when the truth is it can be really hard and extremely time consuming. But this is what it takes.

After I'd bought four, six, 11+ properties through different agents, on market and off, many of those same agents remembered that I was a serious property investor and would call me randomly from month to month with new properties they were about to list, especially if the owner was extremely motivated to get a quick sale. Over the years the more my story has become known and shared through media appearances, the more property opportunities I have been presented with. The more agents who know you are serious, the better your chances of securing great property deals, which is why many people today use a property buyer's agent to streamline the process.

Using a buyer's agent

Just as a seller's agent wants to get the best price for the vendor, a buyer's agent wants to get the best price for the buyer. They both use their knowledge of the market and the negotiating and bidding process to get the best deal for their client.

Finding the right investment property at the right price takes time. If you're working crazy hours to get your cash reserves up, as I was when I first started out, you might not have time to go hunting every weekend. You can't afford to waste hours driving across the city to a dead-end option. This is one of the ways a buyer's agent can help. Once they know what you're looking for, they can narrow down the options for you, so you need only go look at properties that tick all your boxes. Furthermore, because they are so well connected in the market, they can sometimes find properties that are right for you that haven't even been advertised.

As my contacts and knowledge grew, it was a natural progression for me to become a buyer's agent. Many people were asking for my help after seeing me in the media and I love getting the best deal for other people as well as for me, so it made sense to make this my job. Nowadays I have a team of buyer's agents that help busy, inspiring property investors to purchase properties of amazing value. When you hire a buyer's agent you get someone with great contacts and great insights who is totally committed to finding you the best property for your investment needs and getting you the best deal possible.

If you love looking at properties and want to do the hunting yourself, you can still use the agent to help you bid at auction or negotiate the best deal. Bidding and negotiating need a cool head, and it can be hard if you don't have the experience. As I've said before, property investors need to take the emotion out of their decision-making. Working with a buyer's agent can help with that. And they know what makes a good investment property. You may think you know what you want, but they can see all the options to ensure you optimise your investment.

If you're getting the full service—from finding to buying the property—the cost of a buyer's agent is usually 1.5 to 2 per cent of the price. It's less (between $10k and $15k depending on their expertise, experience and demand) if you enlist them only for the negotiation or bidding.

A question I'm often asked is why don't I buy all these properties for myself? I've done a string of free YouTube videos answering this and many such questions. The short answer is I couldn't buy every single property even if I wanted to, because of issues with finance. For example, if out of 10 000 jobs we do in a year we close 500 amazing deals. I couldn't buy and hold 500 properties in one year and get finance for them all! Hardly anyone could.

CLIENT EXAMPLES
Nathan

In 2019 Nathan reached out when buying his second investment property. I'd helped him buy his first the year before (he now has three). Nathan is a good friend of mine: we went to high school together, and his goal starting out was very similar to mine. He also grew up in public housing in Mount Druitt, western Sydney, and his family was always struggling with money. He too wanted to get out of the poverty cycle and create long-term wealth.

Nathan was in his late twenties and worked as a panel beater and labourer for a salary of $45 000. He now lives on the Gold Coast. He bought his first property at age 26, and his second and third within two years. He wants to continue to expand his portfolio.

Nathan bought his second investment property in 2019 in Mermaid Waters, Gold Coast, for $287 000 on a 10 per cent deposit. The comparable market price was $330000 to $340000. The property was under market price because it was an off-market urgent sale.

After a rent increase, up to $500 a week, this would offer a 9 per cent yield.

Recent new valuation/comparable sales was $500000 to $550000, an increase of $200000 in two years.

Table 12.3 (overleaf) gives a breakdown of the figures for this property at the time Nathan purchased it.

Over the next two years, during which a tenant moved out and he did a small renovation, growing market demand allowed him to raise the rent substantially. Table 12.4 (overleaf) shows the numbers at the two-year mark.

Nathan proudly shows off his new investment property

(continued)

Table 12.3: calculations for Nathan's property

Estimated expenses	Weekly ($)	Monthly ($)	Annually ($)
Council rates	30.77	123.23	1600.00
Strata fees inc. building insurance	42.31	183.33	2200.00
Water rates	23.08	100.00	1200.00
Building insurance	–	–	–
Management fees	21.15	91.67	1100.00
Mortgage repayments (current interest rate)	153.85	666.67	8000.00
Landlord insurance	5.77	25.00	300.00
Estimated totals	**276.92**	**1200.00**	**14400.00**

Income comparables			
Lower rent	380.00	1646.67	19760.00
Higher rent	420.00	1820.00	21840.00

Estimated cash flow before tax			
Lower rent	103.08	446.67	5360.00
Higher rent	143.08	620.00	7440.00

Table 12.4: Nathan's figures after two years

Estimated expenses	Weekly ($)	Monthly ($)	Annually ($)
Council rates	30.77	133.33	1600.00
Strata fees inc. building insurance	42.31	183.33	2200.00
Water rates	23.08	100.00	1200.00
Building insurance	–	–	–
Management fees	21.15	91.67	1100.00
Mortgage repayments (current interest rate)	153.85	666.67	8000.00
Landlord insurance	5.77	25.00	300.00
Estimated totals	**276.92**	**1200.00**	**14400.00**
Income comparables			
Lower rent	500.00	2166.67	26000.00
Higher rent	550.00	2383.33	28600.00
Estimated cash flow before tax			
Lower rent	223.08	966.67	11600.00
Higher rent	273.08	1183.33	14200.00

Naomi and Jen

In early 2020 Naomi heard about me through social media and my YouTube videos, and reached out for help buying her next investment property. At this point she already had two properties and had been saving steadily to buy more. Naomi and her partner Jen's end goal was to fund a comfortable retirement, as well as to increase their borrowing capacity so they could purchase a home in Sydney as their principal place of residence.

Naomi, in her early thirties, lived in western Sydney and worked at one of the big four banks for $60 000 to $80 000 (their combined income was around $130 000). With my assistance, Naomi bought four more properties within 18 months, all within 35 minutes of Brisbane metro. She now has six properties in her portfolio, which will give her positive cash flow / capital growth for further investing. She found that being time-poor made it hard for her to keep purchasing.

Naomi bought her third investment property in 2020 in Brisbane metro for $148 800 on a 10 per cent deposit. The comparable market price was $170 000 to $180 000. An urgent sale ensured this property was under market price. A rental income of $290 a week gave a yield of more than 9.5 per cent. A new valuation/comparable sales of $200 000 to $220 000 meant an increase of up to $70 000 within 18 months.

Table 12.5 shows a breakdown of the numbers for Naomi's property.

Table 12.5: calculations for Naomi and Jen's property

Estimated expenses	Weekly ($)	Monthly ($)	Annually ($)
Council rates	30.77	133.33	1600.00
Strata fees inc. building insurance	53.85	233.33	2800.00
Water rates	23.08	100.00	1200.00
Building insurance	–	–	–
Management fees	21.15	91.67	1100.00
Mortgage repayments (current interest rate)	69.23	300.00	3600.00
Landlord insurance	5.77	25.00	300.00
Estimated totals	**203.85**	**883.33**	**10600.00**
Income comparables			
Lower rent	275.00	1191.67	14300.00
Higher rent	290.00	1256.67	15080.00
Estimated cash flow before tax			
Lower rent	71.15	308.33	3700.00
Higher rent	86.15	373.33	4480.00

(continued)

Naomi and Jen, proud property investors

Their first Queensland property

Buying my first home: a recent Sydney example

In 2019 I bought my first home to live in (primary place of residence), in western Sydney.

This property was, at that stage, the biggest purchase I had made. Francesca and I were yet to be married, but we were looking for a place between where her parents lived and my mum's place. Mum still lived in Mount Druitt while Francesca's parents lived closer to the CBD, so we picked the Parramatta area. It was geographically logical and was also just within the budget we had to get started with our first home together. Based on our rough borrowing capacity as calculated by our mortgage broker, we had a budget of around $650 000 to $750 000.

Neither of us knew much about this area, so we started going to open homes and doing a lot of driving around to get to know it. We finally reached the point that I felt ready, based on deposit and finances, to start making offers. One weekend we went to about a dozen open homes and were just about ready to give up and go home. We noticed that one of the last places on our list was on the way, so we thought we'd quickly get it over and done with.

While inspecting all these properties, in the back of my mind I was always thinking we would probably live there for only two to three years maximum, then we'd upgrade and buy a bigger, nicer home. I always thought that once that happened we'd keep the house and add it to our portfolio.

When we arrived at the front of the house, my first thought was, *shit, that's huge!* It was a very old, brick-clad, double-storey house, with poorly maintained trees and gardens, on a large corner block, which I later learned was just under 600 square metres. It looked as though one of the previous owners had added the second level. It had a pool, a huge balcony and a mostly built granny flat (it just needed the bathroom to be completed). We counted six bedrooms inside the house itself, though one was fully enclosed and was therefore described as a study. The granny flat outside had an additional two bedrooms, for a total of eight! The listed asking price was $749 900, which (based on comparable sales) made it already massively undervalued.

We walked through every room of the property with the agent, and I could tell Fran was as keen on this one as I was. The place needed a lot of work, but I could see how much potential it had. Even in the market at the time, it seemed to me that with cosmetic renovations, and if it was better presented and marketed, this property could be sold for well over $900 000, if not close to $1 million. Many of the great features hadn't been included in the marketing and photos, such as emphasising the corner block and side access, the size of the block and the proximity to the park and Parramatta CBD. The property was hugely under-advertised, with poor photos taken at bad angles in terrible lighting.

Standing there in the kitchen, I placed a verbal offer on the spot of $725 000, and the agent said he'd get back to me that night after speaking with the owner.

While driving home, I checked the RP Data reports and found that the property had previously been advertised as in the

$880000 to $950000 range and had only recently been dropped to $749000. The owners were apparently eager to sell, as they had found another place and needed to settle this one so they could purchase the new one.

RP Data put the range of value as between $775000 and $925000, with a midpoint estimate of $850000, which was the median house price for the suburb, with some renovated duplexes recently selling for $720000 and some much newer, much nicer, five-bedroom houses fetching $1.3 million.

Later that night the agent called back and said there had been multiple offers that day. After some back-and-forth negotiation we ended up signing the contract the next day for $740000.

The day the Sold sticker went up

Before renovation

The next year Francesca and I got married. We lived in this house as we did the renovations inside and out. I cut down all the trees and shrubs. We painted inside and out, put in new carpet and turned the study into the sixth bedroom.

Less than ten months later we got a bank valuation, which came back at $910 000. Now, an important thing to understand about this was that it was a desktop valuation, meaning a valuer didn't come out and see how much better it looked. So we didn't even need to spend the thousands of dollars on renovations! In early 2021 we had it valued again, and it was now worth $1.25 million!

This property was one of my personal favourite purchases. It was around the time of the federal election and many investors were scared that negative gearing was going to be scrapped if there was a change of government, which would have changed the housing market and possibly sent prices down. While other people sat on the fence, I took action, remembering Warren Buffett's words: 'Be fearful when others are greedy and greedy when others are fearful.'

In less than 10 months the property value had increased by almost 25 per cent, which we then used to springboard into another investment property. This is the power of knowing the median price of the suburb, how much each type of property is selling for and what the market trends are.

Here's what the property looks like now.

After renovation, and now worth over $1.2 million

A year after buying and living in this house, Fran and I upgraded to another property and rented this one out for $700 a week. Based on the purchase price of $740 000, this meant a gross yield of 4.91 per cent, which to this day is the lowest yield we have accepted.

That said, I knew from the beginning that this was an 'equity play', buying under market value with huge capital growth potential. Also, once we finished the granny flat we could rent that out for about $350 a week and the main house for $600 minimum, so the weekly rental income could be $950 to $1000. This would then be a maximum rental return of 7.02 per cent, which would make it massively positive geared.

As you can see from the following cash flow sheet, on an interest-only loan of 2.8 per cent it is still positively geared.

Table 12.6 shows how the numbers stacked up.

Table 12.6: calculations for our first home

Estimated expenses	Weekly ($)	Monthly ($)	Annually ($)
Council rates	28.85	125.00	1500.00
Strata fees inc. building insurance	–	–	–
Water rates	23.08	100.00	1200.00
Building insurance	15.38	66.67	800.00
Management fees	34.62	150.00	1800.00
Mortgage repayments (current interest rate)	346.15	1500.00	18000.00
Landlord insurance	8.65	37.50	450.00
Estimated totals	**456.73**	**1979.17**	**23750.00**
Income comparables			
Lower rent	700.00	3033.33	36400.00
Higher rent	800.00	3466.67	41600.00
Estimated cash flow before tax			
Lower rent	243.27	1054.17	12650.00
Higher rent	343.27	1487.50	17850.00

As this property is a house on a corner block and just about every corner block near Parramatta has now been knocked down and replaced with two or three residences—typically a front house and a duplex at the back or vice versa—we may pursue a similar development in the future. But for now the cash flow based on a mid-2 per cent bank interest rate covers itself and we can continue to hold this property for future capital growth, use the equity gain to invest further, and watch the property pay itself off over the next 15 to 25 years.

CHAPTER 13

How to buy a property

Once you've done all your research and have found a property you like, it's time to put in an offer. If you've bought a property before, you'll be familiar with this process and can jump straight to the next and final chapter, where I explain how I manage my properties. If you've never bought a property before, though, it can be confusing the first time, so read on to learn the process step by step.

Your conveyancer

Once you're ready to put in an offer, it's time to engage your conveyancer, who will step you through the process from a legal perspective. Each state in Australia does things a little differently. In Victoria, for example, a document called a section 32 outlines all you need to know about the property, title and associated costs. Other states use other documents, so always check which is relevant in the state in which you are buying.

The offer process

The process of submitting offers and counteroffers can vary depending on whether the property is being sold as a private sale or under auction.

Private sales

If you want to make an offer on a property, the agent will prepare a document for you to sign before presenting it to the vendor. The vendor will either:

- accept the offer

- reject the offer

- make a counteroffer.

If you receive a counteroffer, your options are to:

- accept the counteroffer

- reject the counteroffer and walk away

- continue to negotiate.

Most sellers want a quick sale, and it's in their interest to accept your offer as soon as possible. It's possible to withdraw your offer at any time prior to their acceptance. If they accept the offer, you will be asked to sign a contract agreeing to the purchase.

If you receive a counteroffer, give something back to the vendor. This can be by improving your terms to make it more attractive to them. You can also give the impression that your offer is your final, walk-away offer. Given how strong the market is in most capital cities, you are likely to be competing with other interested buyers, so don't waste too much time going back and forth. Try to be the first person to offer and set up the negotiations so you have the last right of reply with the agent.

Auctions

If you have never attended an auction before, I recommend going along to a few to get a feel for how they work before taking part in one. Auctions can be a good way to purchase property, but there are a few things you need to consider before going down this road. For instance, you can usually make an offer on a property before the auction date, but this is not always the case. Laws surrounding auctions differ from state to state.

When buying at auction, you cannot stipulate any conditions on the purchase of the property, such as buying subject to a building inspection, the sale of your own property or arranging finance. The contract conditions are set at the time of auction, so it is important to get all relevant documents from the agent prior to the auction so your solicitor or conveyancer can take a look and ensure you understand the conditions outlined in the contract.

If your bid is successful, you will sign the contract immediately after the auction and won't be given the opportunity to review the terms and conditions formally. Usually the only room for negotiation will be around the settlement date.

If the final bid falls short of the reserve, the property may be passed in. The highest bidder may then enter negotiations with the agent immediately following the auction. Alternatively, the vendor may agree to sell at this lower price, at which time the property is said to be 'on the market' and the auctioneer may attempt to extract more bids prior to making the sale.

How to communicate your offer in a private sale

It's common practice to communicate your offer in writing or over the phone. I usually put a 48-hour time limit on the offer, so they know they have to decide quickly whether or not to accept it.

Offers are usually made with a few subject to's. For example, most people make an offer subject to a pest and building inspection (if you don't, you could be buying a structurally unsound house without realising it, and therefore massively overpaying). It's common also to make an offer subject to finance.

Here's an example of an offer:

Regarding property at [address], I offer $405 000, subject to a pest and building inspection, and subject to finance. My settlement terms are flexible — anywhere from 30 to 90 days.

Negotiating a better price

You may have been wondering while reading this book how I managed to get such great prices on most of my purchases. The truth is, *I learned how to negotiate.*

Successful negotiation is an art that requires patience, understanding and a certain level of tact. The more experience you get, the more confident you will become, which will help you achieve excellent results. It's a skill that will serve you well in many areas of your investment journey, and in your life in general, so it's worth taking some time to learn how to do it properly.

Here are some of my key points for negotiating a bargain investment property.

Remember that negotiation is a process

Negotiating successfully requires you to understand that it is a two-way street. Both buyer and seller have goals they wish to achieve from the transaction, so you should be ready for a little give and take in order to strike a deal.

Assess the seller's situation

Putting yourself in the seller's shoes can help you to figure out their motivation for selling, and to use that to promote the virtues of your case. Good negotiators in the property world will find properties that need to be sold quickly for various reasons. These motivated sellers I refer to as 'D' or 'distress' vendors, who may be selling for any of the following reasons:

- death
- divorce
- debt (or financial hardship)
- deadline
- distance
- disaster.

Ask questions

Skilled negotiators ask many questions, both to seek out D vendors and to determine whether the property is worth bargaining for.

Here are some good questions to start with:

- Why is the vendor selling?
- Have they purchased another property?

- What settlement terms are preferred?

- How long have they owned it?

- Is it an investment or owner occupied?

- Is it tenanted?

- Have they had any offers?

- How long has it been on the market?

- Is the vendor testing the market?

The answers you receive should help you build a strategy and plan your next move, or decide to walk away and focus your efforts elsewhere.

Know the market

The price you are personally willing to pay for the property is only part of the equation. It is important to thoroughly research current, comparable sales prices for similar properties in the area, and to assess the current level of demand for those properties.

Be confident

A confident and positive attitude goes a lot further than you might think towards making a strong impression and creating goodwill between you and the agent. Going into a negotiation feeling prepared, well researched and optimistic will help you overcome any fears and niggling self-doubt. You've got this!

Use the agent

In most cases, the seller will be using a real estate agent. I recommend you conduct all negotiations through the agent and avoid the temptation to talk directly with the owner, even if they contact you. Agents are more experienced and less likely to have an emotional attachment to the property or the situation behind the sale.

Be open and respectful

Open, honest and clear communication throughout the process will help you to achieve a better result and build a trusting relationship with the agent and seller. Resist game playing, such as hiding your interest in the property, as this can backfire and result in an agent not taking you seriously. Let them know your intentions early on.

Know your limits

Buying property can be an emotional experience for all parties. Be aware of your upper purchase limit and stick to it. It is all too easy to allow yourself to get caught up in the excitement of a purchase. It's okay to walk away sometimes—there will always be another property out there for you.

Present your offer carefully

There are a number of strategies you can use when presenting your initial offer, ranging from offering your highest and final price straight up, or starting low and giving yourself lots of room to move. Your strategy will be influenced by the circumstances of the sale and the seller.

Think through low offers

There are times when making a ridiculously low offer in the hope that the seller is naïve or desperate for a sale will pay off, but it can often get negotiations off to a bad start. To save time and heartache, and if you are genuinely keen on the purchase, you should offer something close to your final expectations. The seller will be interested or not, and you are free to walk away and try again elsewhere.

If you make a legitimate low offer, it is important to present a case for why the lower price is justified. For example, the property might need some repairs or renovation, be located next to a busy road or have been on the market for a while.

Gauge the competition

You can gauge interest in the property by asking the agent how many contract requests, repeat inspections and building reports there have been on the property. Knowing how many other interested parties there may be can help you tailor your strategy.

Organise a pest and building inspection

Once an offer is accepted, you should quickly organise a pest and building inspection. This is as simple as googling for P&B inspectors in the area, contacting a few for quotes and choosing one. They will inspect the property (at a time agreed with the seller and agent), and check it for any significant building concerns or pest problems. They will then write a report for you, itemising their findings. Sometimes a serious issue will be identified and can be grounds for the buyer to back out of the deal, or to negotiate a lower price that takes account of the costs that will be incurred in fixing the issue.

Organise your loan

As soon as the offer is accepted you will contact your bank to begin the process of getting your mortgage approved. (Chapter 10 includes detailed information on the different mortgage options available to you.) Completing the paperwork always involves some effort, but once the loan is formalised, the house is yours! The contract goes unconditional and the only thing left is settlement, which the conveyancer and your bank will organise. Just make sure you have the required funds in your account by settlement.

Finding a tenant

Once settlement has occurred, you can contact the agent you've chosen to manage the property, and let them know it's ready for listing as a rental. The agent will hold inspections, collect rental applications, and give them to you with their recommendation of who to select. You choose your renter, and *voilà*! You have an investment property bought and tenanted.

Another great example from 2020

I picked up this property in Queensland during the pandemic. It was an off-market opportunity brought to my attention by a real estate agent I had known for years. Whenever she has an owner who needs an urgent sale she lets me know, and if the property passes my criteria I begin to negotiate to see if we can get it to a price where there is so much value I can't possibly turn it down!

This bargain was a two-bedroom, low-set townhouse roughly 30 minutes from Brisbane's CBD. It was on roughly 200 square metres, with a garage and a low-maintenance backyard area. I managed to negotiate it down to $133 000. At the time it was rented out for $280 a week, giving a gross yield of 10.9 per cent!

Table 13.1 (overleaf) shows how the numbers stacked up.

Anyone could buy this property — on a 5 per cent deposit it would need only about $8000!

Table 13.1: calculations for a 2020 lowset townhouse purchase

Estimated expenses	Weekly ($)	Monthly ($)	Annually ($)
Council rates	28.85	125.00	1500.00
Strata fees inc. building insurance	42.31	183.33	2200.00
Water rates	25.00	108.33	1300.00
Building insurance	–	–	–
Management fees	21.15	91.67	1100.00
Mortgage repayments (current interest rate)	69.23	300.00	3600.00
Landlord insurance	5.77	25.00	300.00
Estimated totals	**192.31**	**832.33**	**10 000.00**
Income comparables			
Lower rent	280.00	1 213.33	14 560.00
Higher rent	290.00	1 256.67	15 080.00
Estimated cash flow before tax			
Lower rent	87.69	380.00	4 560.00
Higher rent	97.69	423.33	5 080.00

Here's a numbers breakdown of the different deposit percentage options for this property:

5% deposit	$6 650
Stamp duty	$3 500
Legal fees and pest & building report	$2 000
Miscellaneous buffer expenses	$2 000
Lenders mortgage insurance	$4 000
Total (rough figure)	**$18 200**

10% deposit	$13 300
Stamp duty	$3 500
Legal fees and pest & building report	$2 000
Miscellaneous buffer expenses	$2 000
Lenders mortgage insurance	$4 000
Total (rough figure)	**$24 800**

20% deposit	$26 600
Stamp duty	$3 500
Legal fees and pest & building report	$2 000
Miscellaneous buffer expenses	$2 000
Total (rough figure)	**$34 000**

In this instance I paid a 20 per cent deposit. It wasn't my preference, but the larger your portfolio the riskier you appear to banks, which means the harder it becomes to get finance. Even if your properties are incredible investments with the best possible returns, the investor is still holding debt. The more debt investors have, the riskier they appear to banks.

An important thing to note about this purchase is the annual strata fees of $2200. Most new investors are put off properties that have body corporate or strata fees, thinking it's too expensive, but if the property still has a high yield, why should it matter? Remember, all you're looking for is properties that fit the key three criteria. Many people don't realise that the strata amount often includes building insurance (which was true of this property). It also covers maintenance of the common areas, general structural integrity, and things like gutters and roofs.

I got this property for an amazing price. Comparable sales for properties in the complex were $175 000 (on 24 March 2014) and $229 000 (on 8 August 2017).

So how on earth did I get it for $133 000? Here are the main reasons:

- My connections with dozens of different real estate agents ensure they bring urgent/distressed properties and highly motivated vendors to my attention.

- I was investing in the Brisbane property market during COVID, when many buyers were sitting on the fence.

- The property had minor issues that would scare off many investors. The pest and building report noted some cracks in the ceiling, signifying slight building movement, along with the usual cosmetic issues that arise with any property over 10 years old: cracked tiles, older carpet, a new vanity needed, new taps and washers needed. I probably spent about $4000 fixing these things (all tax deductions!).

- The owner was desperate to sell because of financial circumstances, though I never found out the exact reason. (Many prospective investors get hung up on asking why the owner is selling. I agree it's important to ask, but sometimes they'll ask the agent to keep it private. And does it really matter why they're selling? A good deal is a good deal.)

Remember, opportunities like this arise every week!

CHAPTER 14

How to manage your properties

Once you've bought your property you need to stay on top of managing it. This includes managing the income and expenditure, fulfilling your obligations as a landlord by making sure it's well maintained and keeping on top of your tax. I do this for 30 properties, which may sound like a mammoth task, but once you understand how it works and set up a system, it's really pretty easy.

Property managers

At the start of my journey I tended to micro-manage my property managers, and looking back I recognise this was a big mistake. I should have been focused on finding the next great property deal, and where I could make the next $100000, rather than squandering my time sourcing the best quotes to replace a tenant's air conditioner costing around $1500.

I find that many investors are too focused on maintaining what they have rather than growing their property portfolio. Changing this mindset took me years to achieve. It's about learning the true value of your time and what you should most profitably focus on.

Rental property managers can do the lion's share of the property administration. I have arranged for all bills, such as rates and strata fees, to be sent directly to my rental property managers, who pay them from the rental income received. They also organise all the quotes for maintenance and repairs, and if the job is under $500 they have the discretion to get it fixed without checking in with me.

A good property manager will:

- set and handle rent
- market for and screen tenants
- handle tenancy issues
- schedule and track maintenance of the property
- organise quotes for repairs, replacements and other expenses
- manage finances and records
- organise insurances for the property, such as building and landlord insurance
- review rental increases over the years.

My property managers send me monthly statements, which itemise all the property expenses, and an end-of-financial-year statement. Probably the biggest task is sending all the statements, bank statements and invoices at tax time, but I usually can get this done within three to six hours, and it's only once a year.

Tax accountants charge between $100 and $200 to do the tax return for each property, and some of them give discounts, so my last bill for my tax return was between $2000 and $3000.

Managing lots of mortgages at once has now become second nature to me. My 30 properties are split across seven lenders, meaning roughly four properties for each lender. I have one account with each of these banks to manage the income, expenses and mortgage payments for the properties at that bank, so I'm really only managing seven accounts for my 30 properties. I have a buffer in each of these accounts that will cover four to five months' repayments, just in case anything goes wrong.

I'm not obsessive about interest rates, I look at them only about once a year to check if I can get lower rates. My focus is on expanding the portfolio rather than getting the lowest rate possible, although of course this could change in the future.

Tax deductions

Understanding all the possible tax deductions will help you get the most out of your investment property or portfolio. If you are not using an accountant, you should go to the ATO website for the absolute latest update on what you can deduct, because it can change. But to give you an idea, here's a list of things you can claim for your rental property—as long as you have proof of payment. Remember to keep your receipts!

Loan interest

This is the biggest deduction you can claim on your rental property. Because you've used the loan to generate an income, the interest you pay on the loan is tax deductible.

Rental expenses

Any expenses you accrue in getting your property listed and rented out, then administering and maintaining it, are tax deductible. These include:

- rental agent fees, including any setup costs such as advertising and photography from when you first listed it

- council rates

- owners' corporation fees

- insurance, including property insurance and landlord insurance

- any utility bills you pay, such as water bills in apartment blocks that don't have separately metered bills, or if utilities are included in the rent

- any repairs and maintenance—note this is only for maintaining at the current standard, not for improving the value

- gardening—maintenance and replacement only, not landscaping improvements that will increase the property value

- cleaning costs if regular cleaning is part of the agreement with the tenant, or if the property needs cleaning between tenancies

- pest control

- land tax.

Depreciation

Depreciation relates to the wear and tear of your property, and can be claimed over time and offset against your income from the property. There are two types of depreciation. Plant and equipment depreciation covers fixtures and fittings that eventually wear out (such as carpets, cookers, and air con systems). Capital works depreciation covers any construction that commenced after 16 September 1987 or any renovations. Check with an accountant and speak to a quantity surveyor to find out the potential depreciation benefits for a specific property.

Quantity surveyor

When you buy your property you can get a quantity surveyor to create a depreciation schedule. The fees for the quantity surveyor are also tax deductible.

Accountant fees, bank charges and administration costs

Managing investment properties is like running a business, so you can claim your accountant's fees and bank charges, as well as any admin costs such as internet, phone and stationery.

CONCLUSION

I hope by now I have persuaded you that achieving your property dreams really is within your reach. It's never 'too late'. You haven't 'missed out' on all the opportunities. You're not 'too old' or 'too young'. You don't have 'too low an income to be able to afford an investment'. The only thing stopping you is your mindset. Are you ready to grow? To take control of your future? To decide that this year, this month, this week, is your time to begin? There is so much potential still in Australia, right now, for people of any age and income to begin building their own property portfolio!

To further inspire you and demonstrate just what is possible, here's another great story.

Ben and Loren

Ben and Loren reached out to me in 2018. They were in their late twenties / early thirties, were engaged and lived in Melbourne, where Ben worked as a sales retail consultant and Loren as a retail store assistant.

They got started in property because they wanted to become financially free at a young age. They didn't want to rely on their working incomes alone. They learned

(continued)

there were lots of benefits to owning property, such as the consistent cash flow from rent, the increase of the properties' value year on year and the tax benefits. Their long-term goal was to build the largest asset base they could, with 100+ properties in their portfolio. Over the next four years they were able to purchase 17 properties! An incredible achievement. Here's what they shared with me about their experience of working with us.

How have you found the experience?

Eddie and the team have been absolutely outstanding! We seriously wouldn't be in the position we're in now without his help. Eddie's guidance and knowledge has given us the confidence to continue to build our position and reach our financial goals. Eddie and the team represent delivery and quality client care.

Successes you have had?

Every property Eddie has secured for us has played a vital role in building our portfolio. He strategically secures properties that allow us to further grow our position by understanding the types of properties we need.

Obstacles/issues you have had to overcome?

Some of the obstacles we had to overcome were personal mindset shifts, and being disciplined with our personal spending. Fear tends to creep in as you continue to expand your portfolio, but with Eddie's guidance and support we've been able to remain focused on our goals and take consistent action.

Here are some of the properties Ben and Loren now own:

Location: Brisbane metro
Rent: 9% yield
Purchase price: $145 000
Eddie helped us secure this deal, which was $30k below market comparable sales.
A well-maintained property 30 minutes from Brisbane CBD.

Location: Brisbane metro
Rent: 8% yield
Purchase price: $167 000
Equity from previous purchases was used to purchase this property, 20 minutes from Brisbane CBD.

Location: Brisbane metro
Rent: 8% yield
Purchase price: $289 000
Eddie helped us secure this property through our SMSF. Great deal with large land size. Eddie's team made purchasing through our SMSF easy and effortless.

Where I'm at now

In 2020 Francesca and I wanted to buy a better house to be our family home for many years to come. We saw this one listed online and loved it, partly because of its location, which was close to family, but our finance wasn't quite ready yet, so we didn't go to the auction. It was near the start of the COVID-19 pandemic, which affected market interest, so when I learned the next day that it hadn't sold at auction I called the agent and made an offer. It was accepted that day.

Looking back, it was an amazing time to buy because the media was putting fear in the property market, which meant we got it for less than it would have cost us during business-as-usual. I'm thankful we pushed forward and took action despite the market jitters. We bought it for $1.28 million and in 2021, after minor renovations (fresh paint and new lighting, fixtures and fittings throughout), we had it revalued at $1.6 million.

One of my bigger purchases, at age 29!

In April 2021, I set myself the goal of buying my mother a house. She was still living in housing commission where I had grown up, which was far from where my wife and I were now living. My property portfolio had reached the point that I could afford to buy her a house.

It was an extremely hot market with all properties receiving multiple offers, so I focused on the area where we lived and checked the online listings hourly to see what was new, as well as calling the local real estate agents to see what listings they had coming up that weren't yet online. I managed to find one around the corner from us.

The property cost $875 000 and was bought over the phone within three hours of its listing for sale. I signed the contract that same day without even walking through the property. I was relying purely on the photos and its location. I knew it would be good for us as a family.

I share this with you to illustrate yet again how the amazing vehicle that is real estate investment can make your financial dreams come true, and help out your family too. Property investing is the way I have built generational wealth and changed my family's circumstances, and I am very grateful to have achieved wealth at this level. This was the 30th property in my personal property portfolio, bought when I was just 29 years old.

Bought a house for Mum, 2021!

Finally, here's a photo of my wife, daughter and me — after all, this is what it's all about.

I wish you the best of luck with your journey. If you want to learn more, feel free to contact me at Dilleenproperty.com.au

Eddie Dilleen

INDEX